AF480174

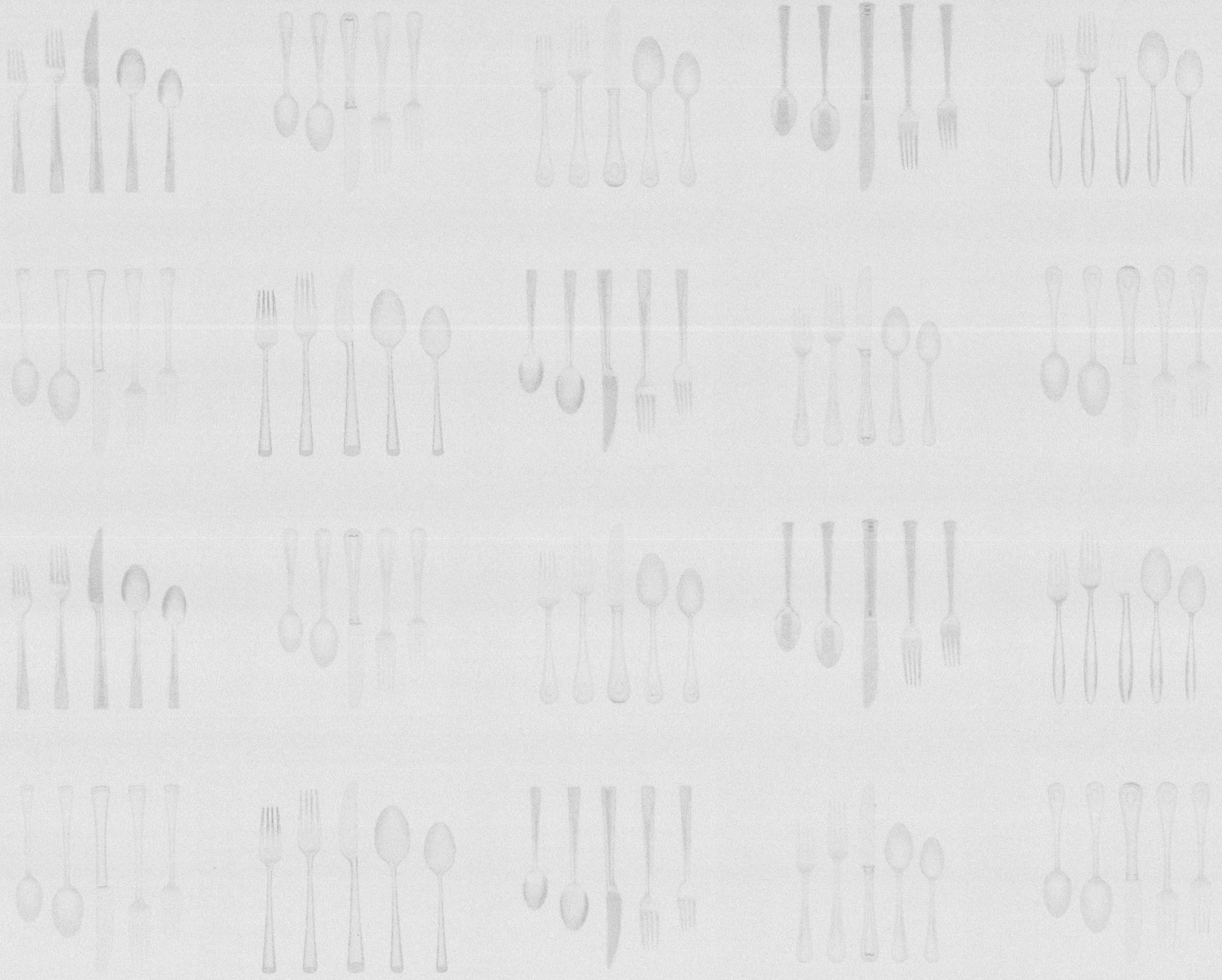

ENTERTAINING *and* CELEBRATING

An Elegant Feast for Every Season

Kristal Damron

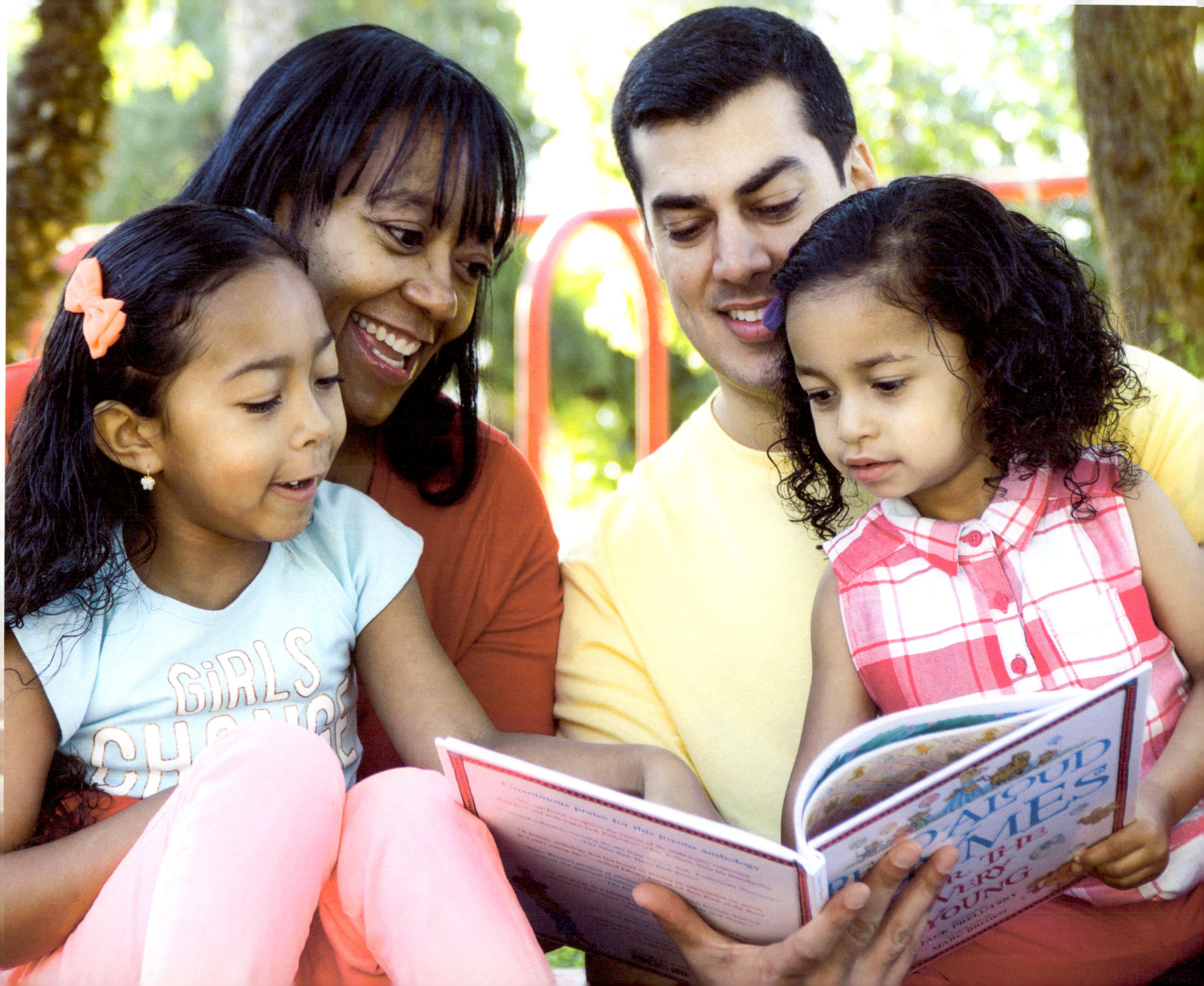

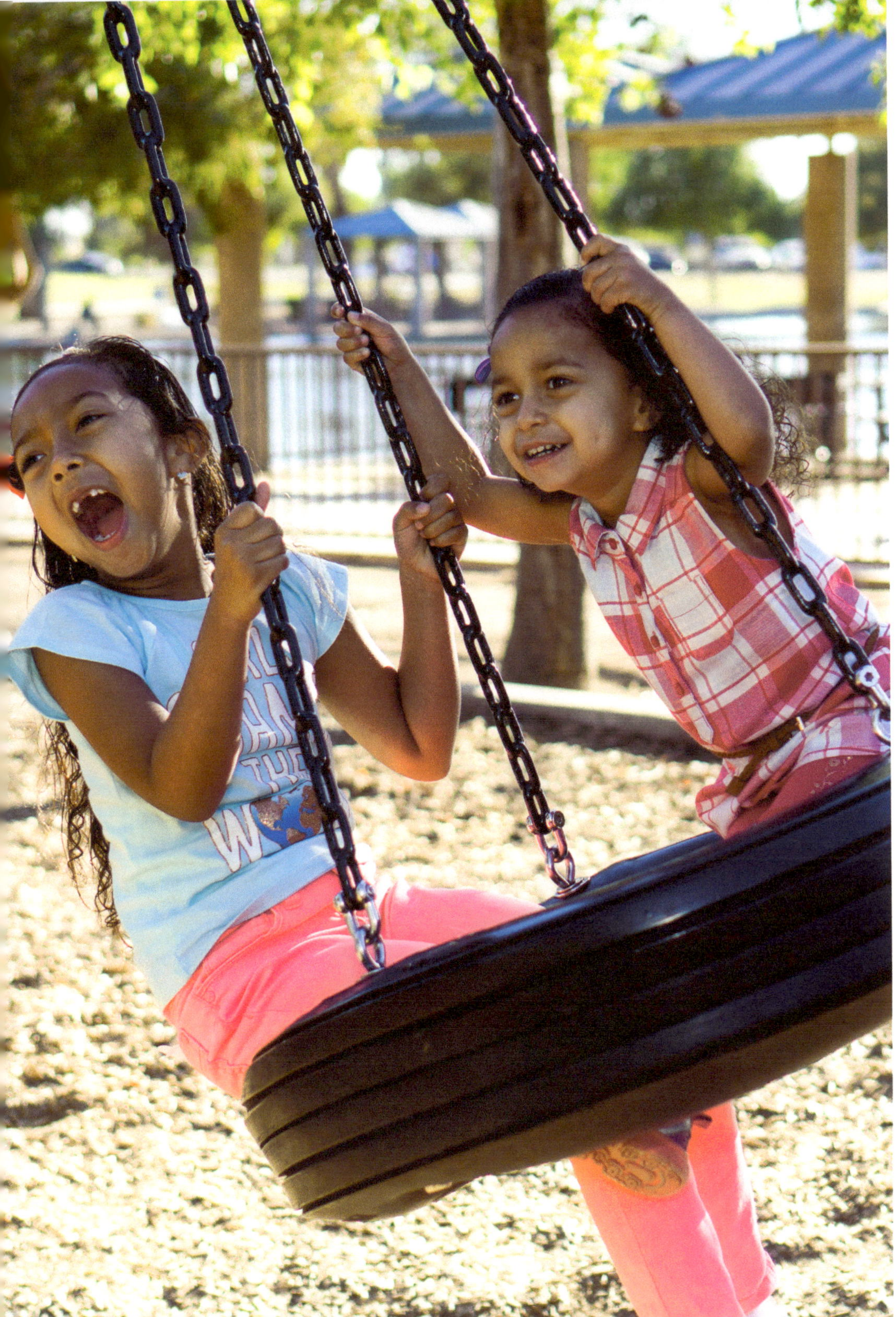

For my darling daughters, Arianna and Alexandria,
Mommy loves you infinitely.

And to my loving and supportive husband,
Jared, you are amazing.

Published by
Reward Your Appetite Catering
Phoenix, Arizona
www.rewardyourappetite.com

ISBN 978-1-7322313-0-6

CONTENTS

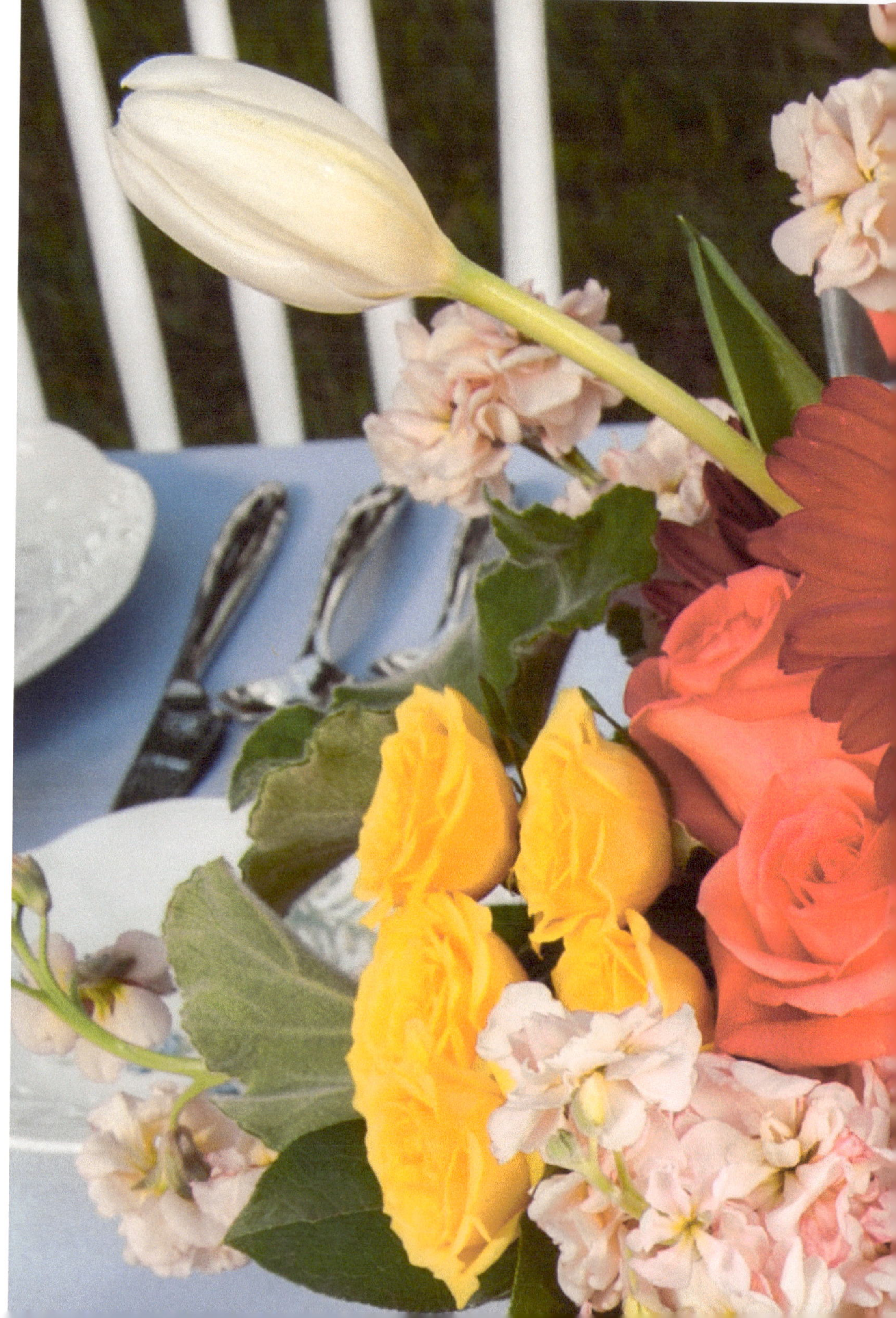

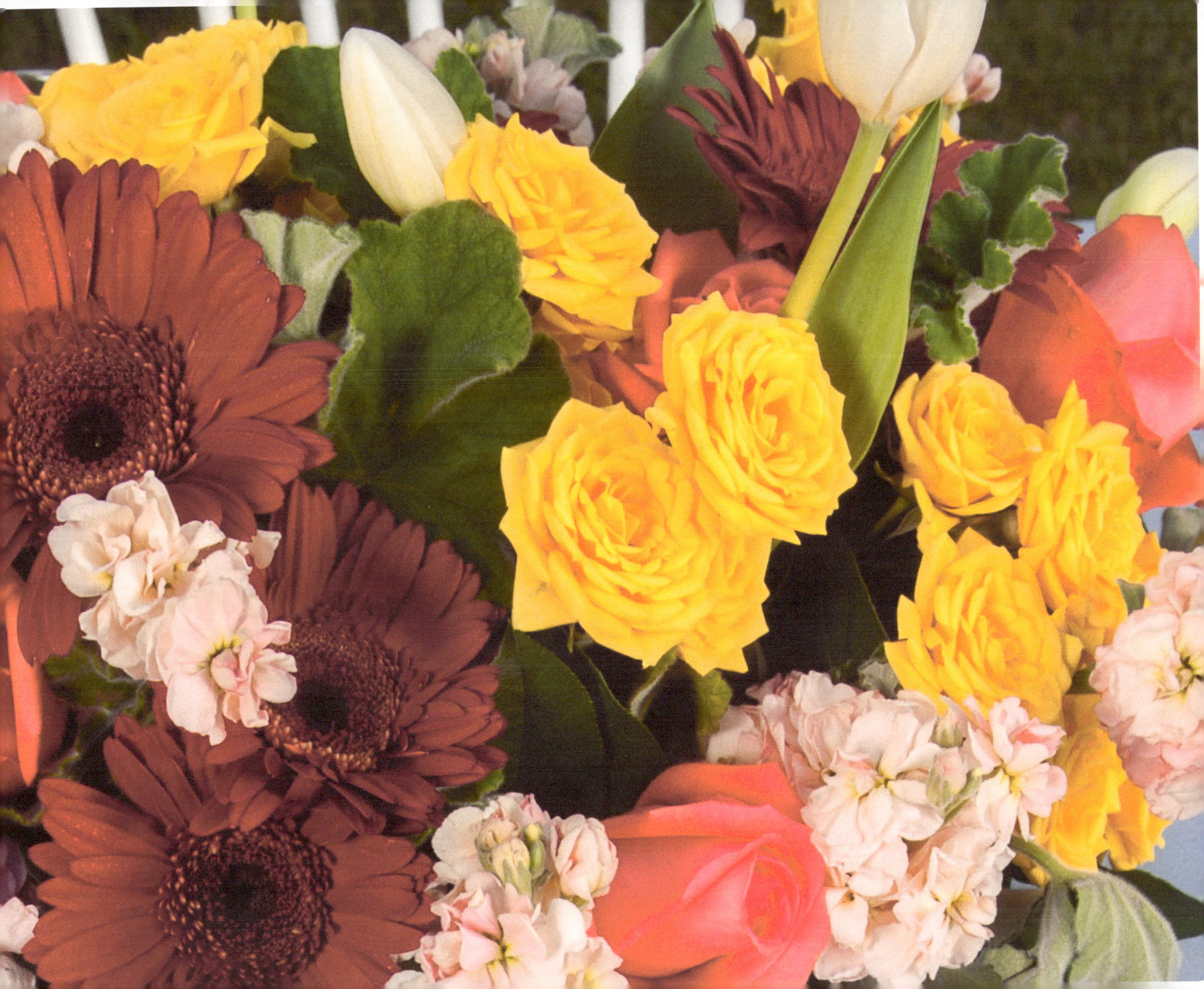

Mommyhood, Catering, Publishing

My three-part journey into Mommyhood, catering, and publishing started when I was pregnant with my first daughter, Arianna Victoria. My work colleagues, who had known me for ten years, told me my life was about to change. I told them, "No it won't. I will still focus on my career in corporate America. I will just tote her on my hip and keep going."

To my surprise, when my daughter arrived, my life did change. Watching my little girl blossom during her first few months of life, I realized I wanted to be available for her, to be "Mommy" instead of hiring help to take my place when I was at work. I wanted to be able to take her to her activities as she grew up, not just hear about what she was doing from the caregivers.

At the same time, I didn't want to give up having a career. Instead, I wanted my time equation to change from spending lots of time in a corporate job to spending lots of time with my family while still working. How could I make this happen?

I am an older mom, so I needed to be strategic in my approach to change. I pondered it, I prayed on it, and the idea of cooking kept coming to mind. I like to cook, and I truly enjoy going to restaurants and having a great meal with wonderful service. I started watching more cooking shows, and more of my conversations with friends were around cooking. The discussion about food, recipes, and preparations had always been commonplace in my life, but I had never thought of a career in cooking or catering before. When I was a child, my grandmother, Emma Jane, would make wonderful meals for the family. She was always trying something new. My cousins and I would be in the kitchen watching her cook and taking notes for recipes.

It was also important to me to have a beautiful setting when dining. As a young adult, I realized my enthusiasm for pretty and inviting surroundings when I had guests over to the house. Activities such as setting the tables, arranging decorations, shopping for ingredients, and planning the events were enjoyable and rewarding. Now the idea of becoming a fine dining caterer and chef started to make sense to me. What would a successful career and business plan for a caterer and chef look like?

My husband, Jared, suggested I take a cooking class to test the waters and see if this is something I would like to do. I took his advice and enrolled in a twelve-week course. It was a great class, and I learned a lot in a short time. Most importantly, my chef instructor had successfully transitioned her own career from the corporate world to the culinary arts, and she was willing to share her story with me.

Listening to how she made this transition gave me insight into how I could do it too—especially how to develop a culinary career without starting as an entry-level cook in a restaurant, which would involve working long days and extensive hours, similar to my corporate experience. As a fine dining caterer, I would have long days too, but I could schedule them when I chose. In addition, I started to learn about other revenue streams related to catering that would help make the career change successful.

So began part two of my journey into catering. Mommyhood is what motivated me to undertake it. Crafting a lifestyle that would allow me to help maintain our quality of life as a family, while providing the flexibility I was seeking, was enough incentive to face my fear of the unknown and try this new adventure. The arrival of my second daughter, Alexandria Isabella, solidified my decision to make this second career a reality.

I decided to take a sabbatical from work. The first step in my business plan was to enroll in culinary school to further my education and to develop my cooking skills.

Then God gave me the idea to write a book. A book? I have never written a book before. The idea for this book came to me in a dream. "You love to entertain. You plan menus for holidays and cater parties for your daughters. You make great food and enjoy setting tables and making everything look beautiful. Write a book about entertaining and celebrating with friends and family."

That idea brought me into the world of publishing—part three of my journey. Now I was exploring two paths—catering and publishing—in parallel. I was combining my zeal for delivering exquisite cuisine and exemplary service with my love for fine dining and elegant table settings with others.

I want to pass on three takeaways I have learned from this experience. First, follow your passion. The road may not be clear, but listen to your inner spirit for guidance. Then create a plan to put that guidance into action. Creating the plan will require some quiet time so you can be of clear mind to write down your thoughts. Be strategic and also flexible.

Second, have courage. Change is difficult at any time. It can be most challenging when it involves stepping away from a comfortable situation where life is good. You might feel you don't have what it takes or your current responsibilities may seem too great for you to initiate change. Your skills may require some polishing or refinement, but you already have what it takes to accomplish whatever you want to do. Fear is just a distraction. Therefore, take the calculated leap of faith and begin. Perseverance can overcome setbacks when you believe in yourself. Even the best-laid plans will have unexpected interruptions, and you will need to adjust to get back on track. Take one step at a time and you will reach your goal.

Third, surround yourself with cheerleaders. These are the people who will support you when your doubts arise. They will give you a big hug when you need it and say the right words to lift your spirits. Following your passion is a journey, and your cheerleaders are there to keep you going until you reach your destination.

Go and be your best!

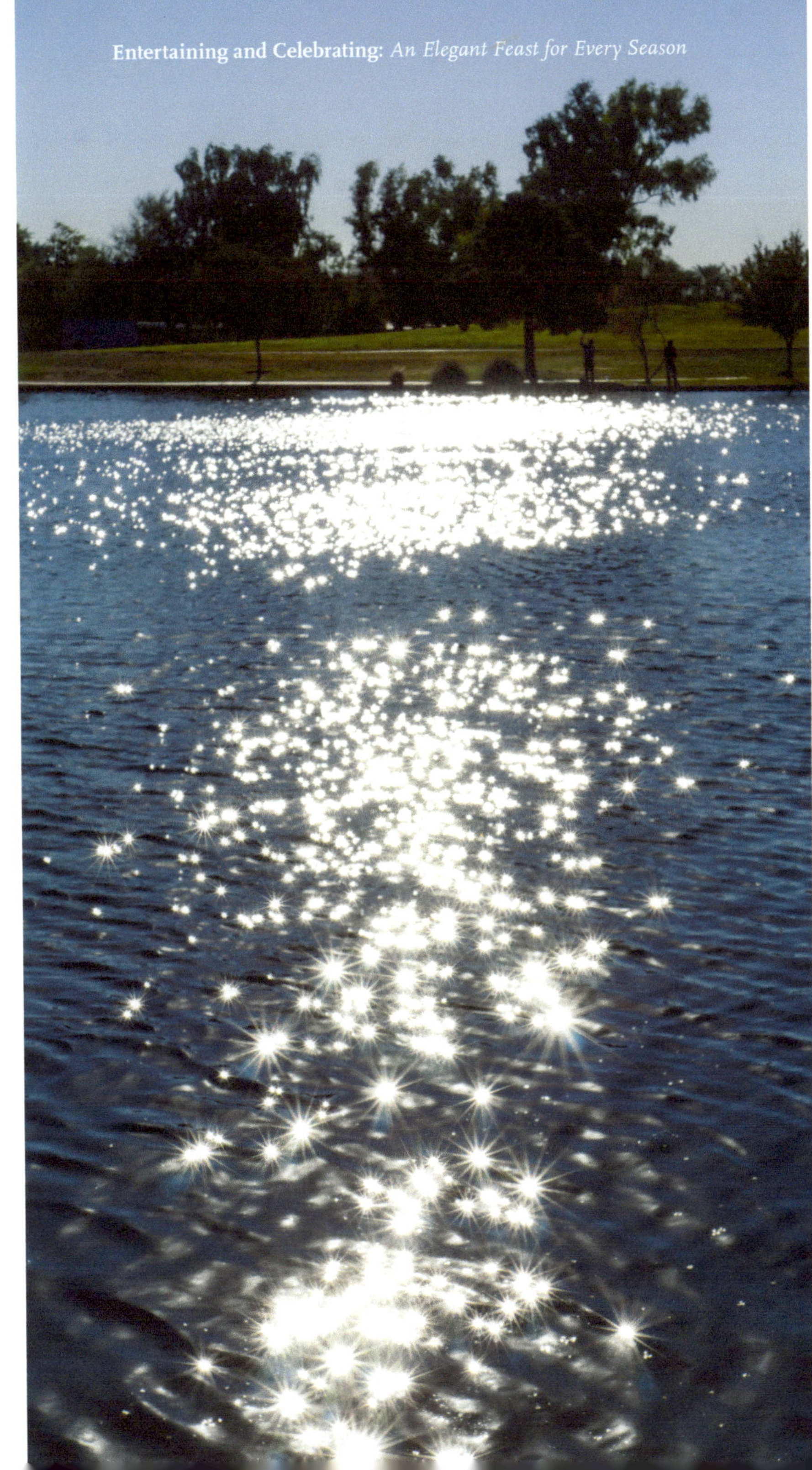

Recapturing Elegance

In the fast-paced complexity of the modern world, many of us have lost the art of slowing down to appreciate the simple pleasures in life. Preparing to entertain is an example: setting the table, creating an ambience, planning the menu and wine, paying attention to the details and beauty of things. Many of us have forgotten these steps and the rush to do other activities has become a priority. As a result, we look for quick, easy fixes and convenience. Or we are unable to visualize how the event should look, and then, we talk ourselves out of planning it.

This flurry of activity can cause us to miss out on beauty, to miss out on elegance. Elegance is harmonious and transcends time. Elegance is unique, a quiet passion, poised and refined. Although elegance is complex at its center, it is displayed simply. Creating elegance involves taking the time to look at the details so you get the result you truly desire. It is the classic invitation that stimulates the imagination and entices guests to attend. It is the careful selection of decorations that satisfies the senses and captures gracefulness and beauty. Cultivating elegance encourages friends and family to enjoy the moment you create for them. To be able to sit together around a stylishly laid table, having a glass of wine, and appreciating each other's company creates lasting memories to cherish year-round. To listen to a person's story and have them listen to yours, rejoicing, laughing, and reducing the stress of your life develops true community.

It can be challenging to come up with ideas for how to create this kind of dining experience. Searching for ideas on the internet can be overwhelming. Therefore, I designed this book as a visual experience with options you can choose to help trigger your own ideas. You can implement the suggested menus and table settings in the book exactly, or you can use them to inspire you to design meals that express your own palate and sense of elegance. You can then target your internet search for specific items you want to add to or change from the menus, table settings, and service recommendations. You can also incorporate your own family and cultural traditions.

The book is organized by season and highlights a specific celebration in each month, drawing from the season's bounty to create an exquisite ambiance and menu. For each celebration, the book showcases an elegant table setting accompanied by chef-prepared four-course menu with wine and cocktail pairings and suggestions on how to serve the cuisine to your guests. These suggestions can be applied at home or in a banquet setting.

You can choose from various table place setting styles—casual, formal, banquet, and breakfast, to name a few—depending on the look and feel you are aiming to achieve. However, being consistent in your approach is important. This applies to service as well. French, English, Russian, and American styles of table service are some of the popular ones. Each is unique and full of cultural history. In the book, I also provide suggestions on dining service styles that complement each month's celebration: family, buffet, action stations, and formal plated. Choose a place setting and a dining service style that is convenient for both the guests and the host.

Bring elegance into the event by taking the time needed to plan and prepare for it. Consider your guests and their palates when designing the menu. Use high-quality ingredients to prepare a meal. For each celebration in this book, I list several dishes that complement each other on a menu or that can be served à la carte. The book includes a pictorial representation of some of the suggested menu items. In order to present the reader with a realistic image of the cuisine the food was not styled or embellished.

The recipes of the various menu items can be found on my website: **rewardyourappetite.com.** With the purchase of this book, five recipes are free to download. Enter code **AVAIR** along with your name and email address.

I encourage you to enjoy your dining experience while entertaining with friends and family. Slow down and recapture elegance, while celebrating life's transitions—season after season, month after month, new beginning after new beginning.

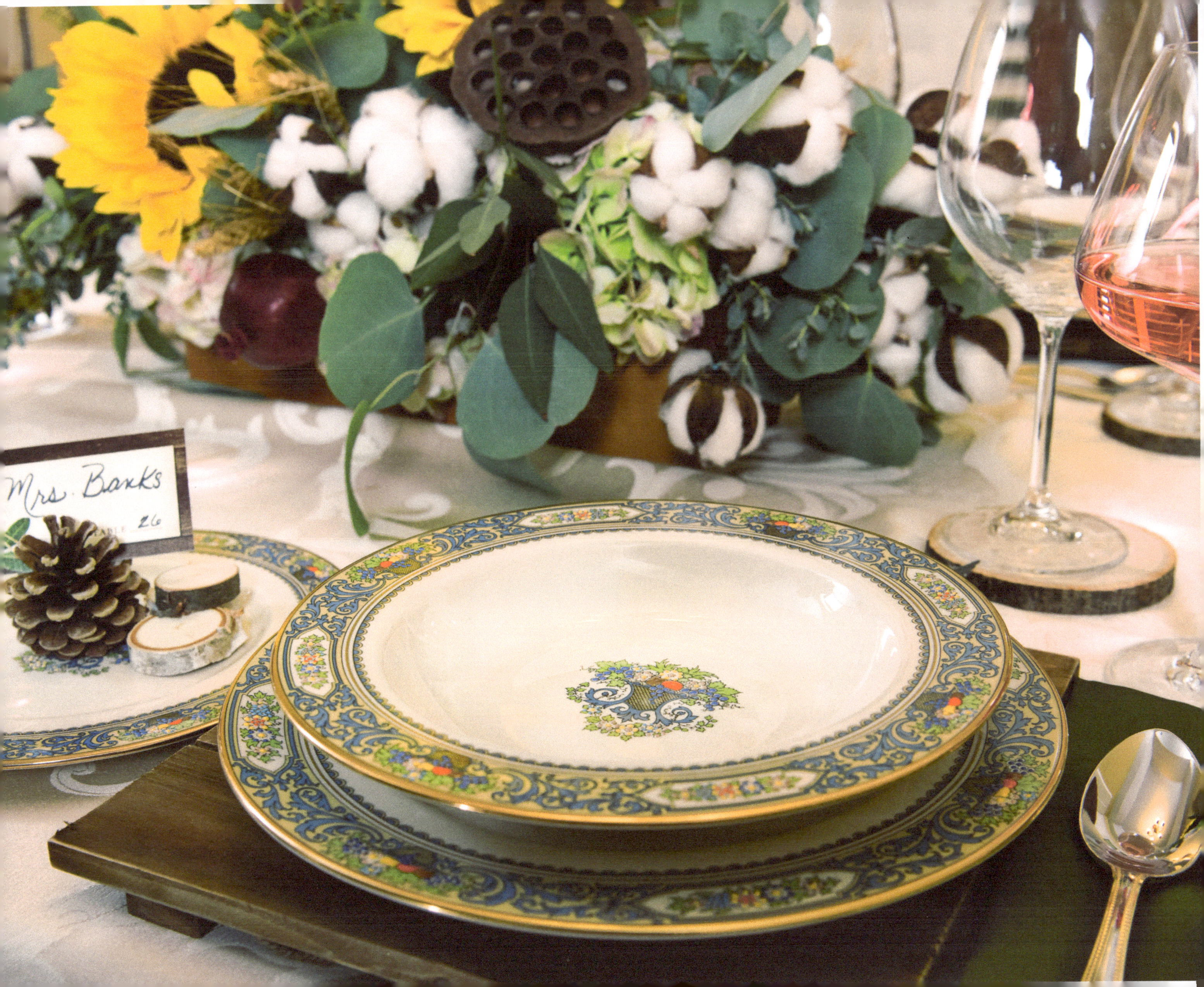
Mrs. Banks
26

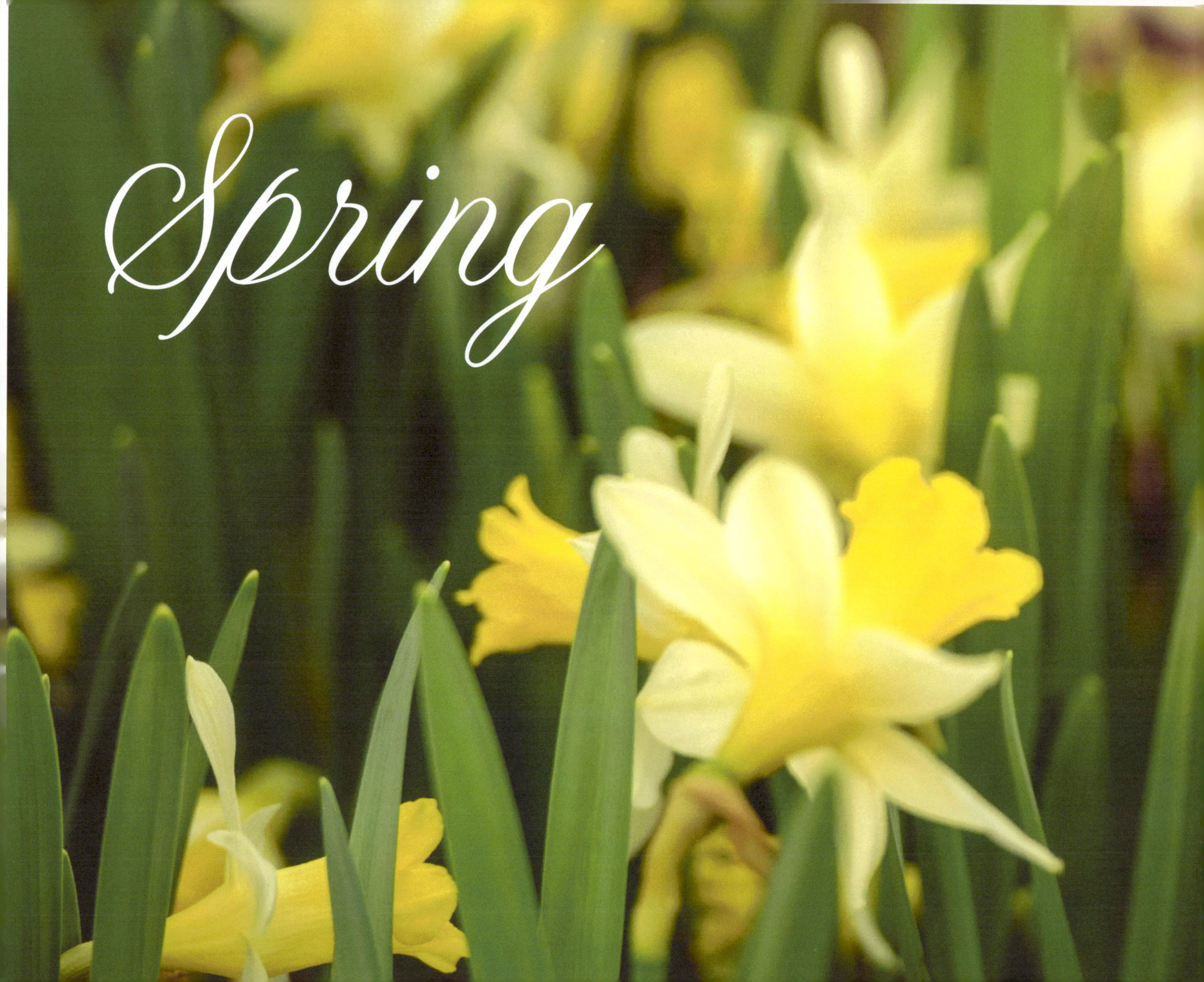
Spring

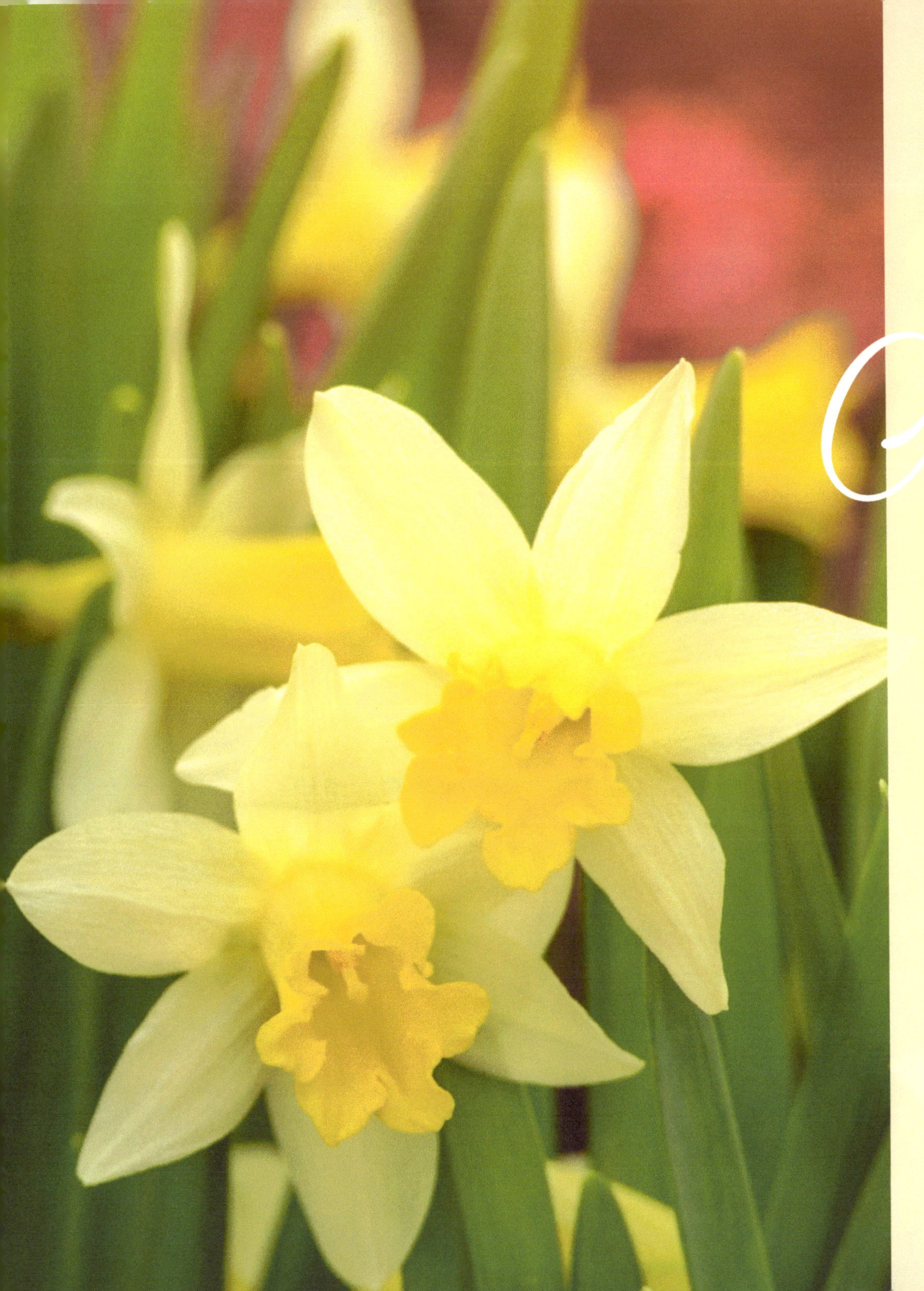

New beginnings, the sweet smell of blossoms in the air, leisurely walks in the meadows as the cool, brisk air awakens your senses to the renewing of life around you. In the springtime, I think of brunch. It's varietal, light, hearty, and full of aromas, with sweet and savory dishes that awaken your palate, leaving a pleasant sensation as you yearn to take the next bite. Spring is one of my favorite times of the year, full of the energy and excitement of new creations happening.

It's a time to look forward to trying new things...embracing change.

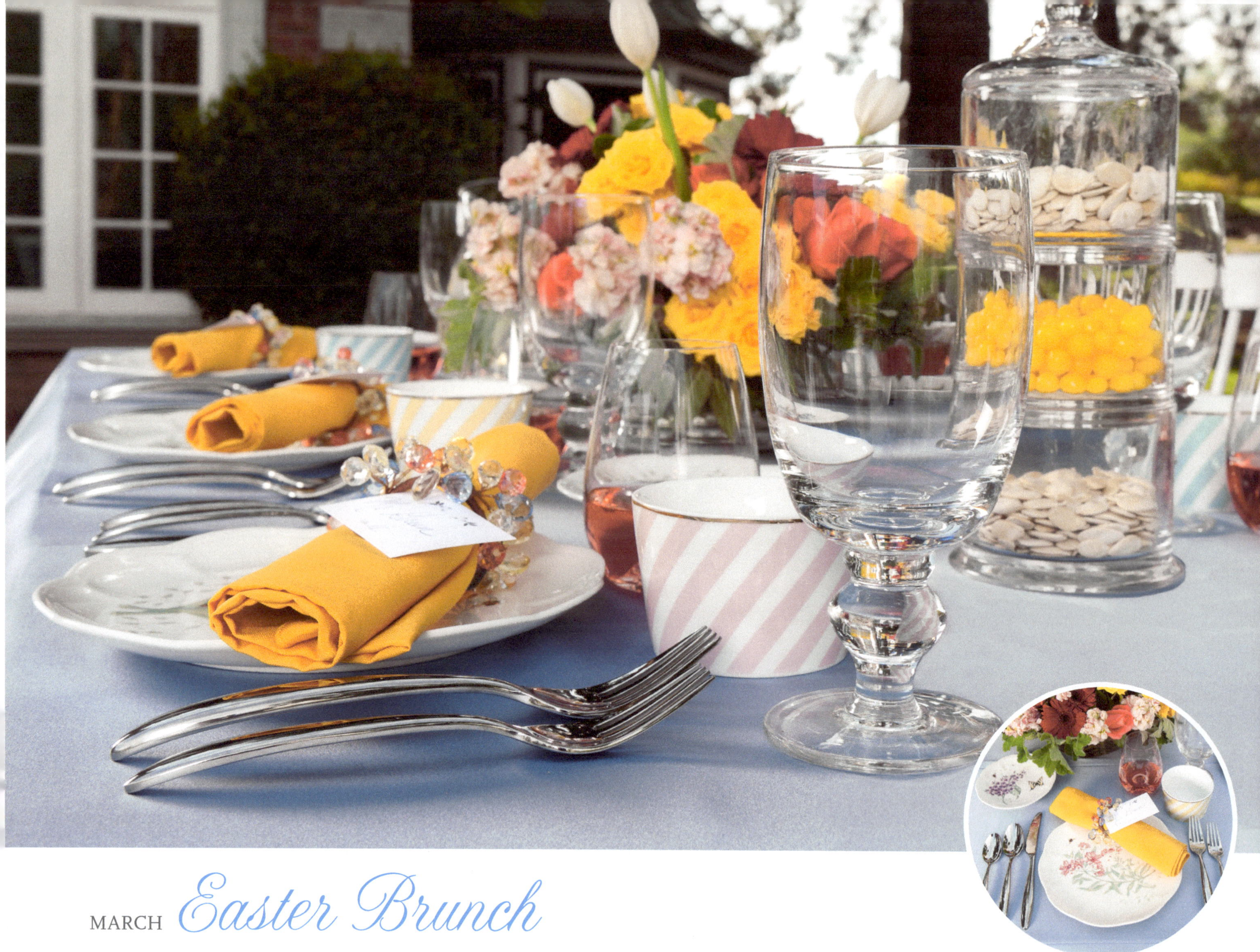

Easter Brunch

In the lush green grass sits an outdoor table set for six, to celebrate Easter and the light touch of the spring breeze.

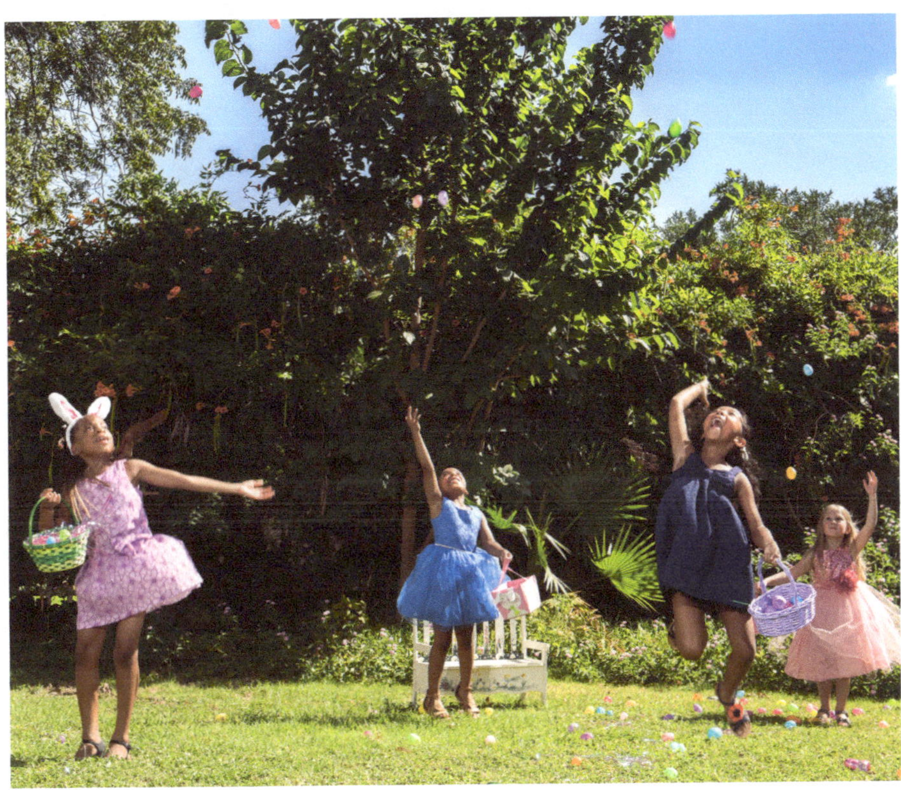

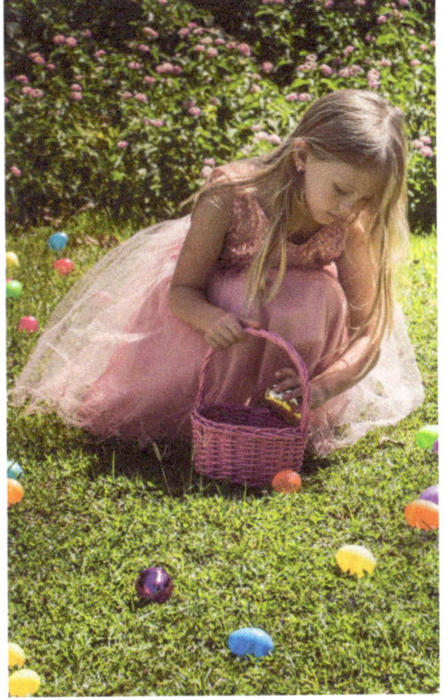

À la Carte Menu

Amuse-bouche
Chocolate Chip Scones | Hazelnut Glaze
Creamy Shrimp Deviled Eggs | Sriracha Crème Fraiche
COCKTAIL PAIRING: *Strawberry Champagne Punch*

First Course: Appetizer
Rainbow Fruit Salad | Vanilla, Citrus Dressing
French Onion Soup | Gruyere Crostini
WINE PAIRING: *Vanilla Puddin Chardonnay*

Second Course: Entrée
Mini Cauliflower Au Gratin | Butter Lettuce
Roasted Red Potatoes | Gorgonzola Compound Butter
Broccoli and Bacon Quiche | Micro Greens
Mini Cucumber Sandwiches | Tuna Tartare
Grilled Ribeye Steak | Butternut Squash White Truffle Butter
WINE PAIRING: *River Road Pinot Noir*
Stephanie's Russian River Valley

Third Course: Dessert
Almond Shortbread Cookie | Chantilly Whipped Cream
Chocolate Mousse | Cointreau & Raspberries
WINE PAIRING: *Dr Heidemanns Doctorberg*
Spatlese Riesling
ASSORTMENT OF TEAS AND COFFEE

Dining Service Style: *Buffet Service with Server Assistance*
Amuse-bouche is served at the table. First, Second, and
Third Course are arranged on serving tables. Guests will
serve themselves from the buffet tables. When their plates
are filled, guests take them to the dining table to enjoy. If
assistance is needed, servers should attend to the guests.
Servers will provide beverage service at tableside.

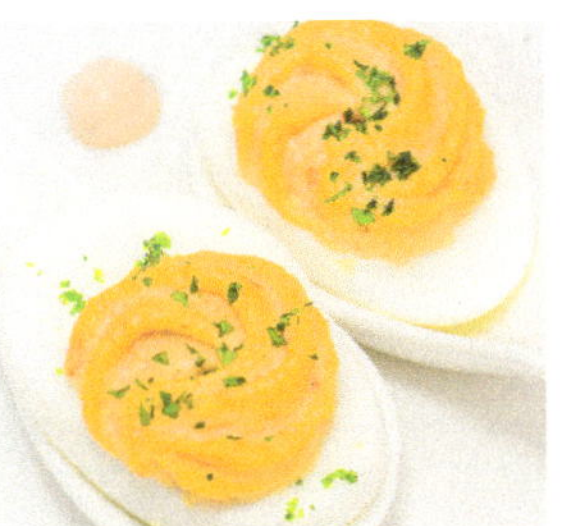

Creamy Shrimp Deviled Eggs

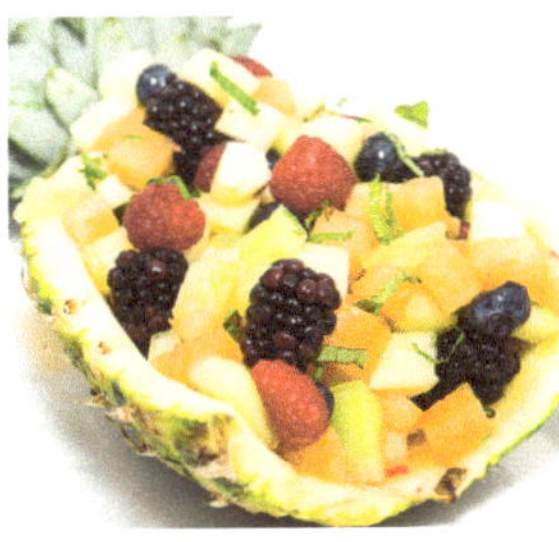

Rainbow Fruit Salad

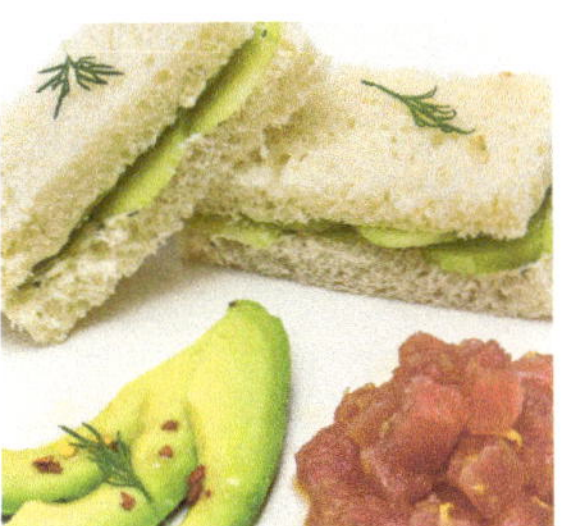

Mini Cucumber Sandwiches

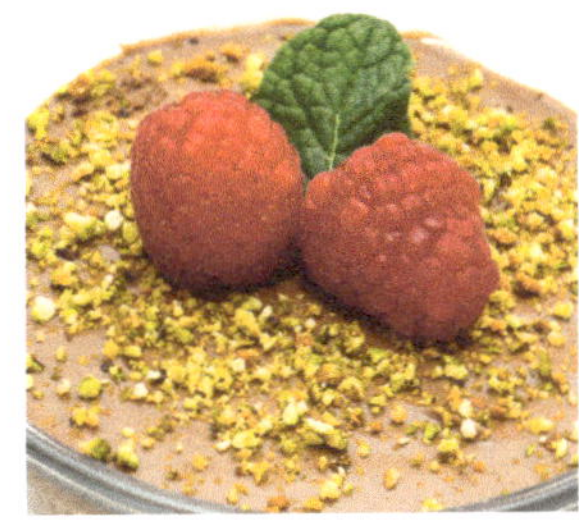

Chocolate Mousse

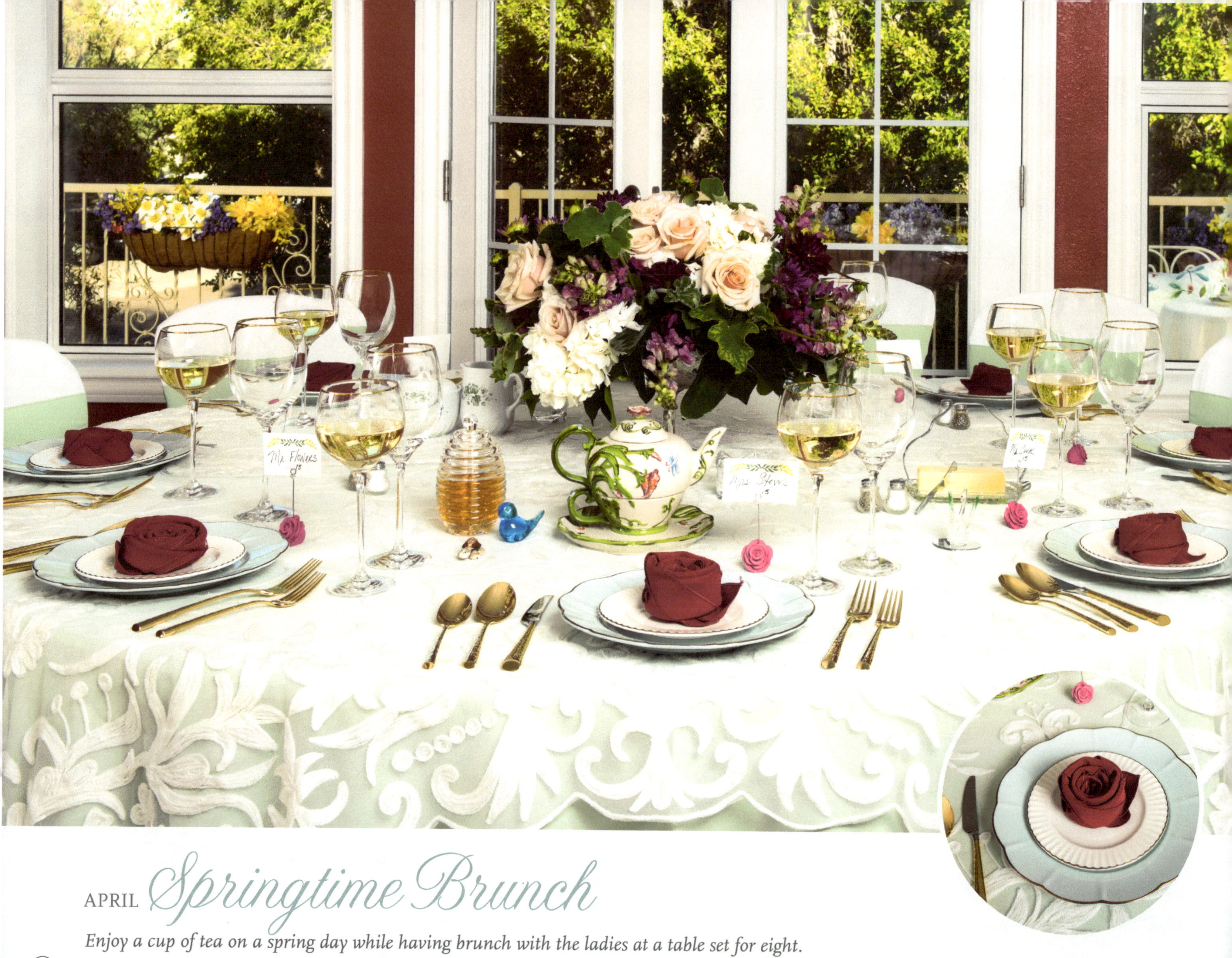

Springtime Brunch

Enjoy a cup of tea on a spring day while having brunch with the ladies at a table set for eight.

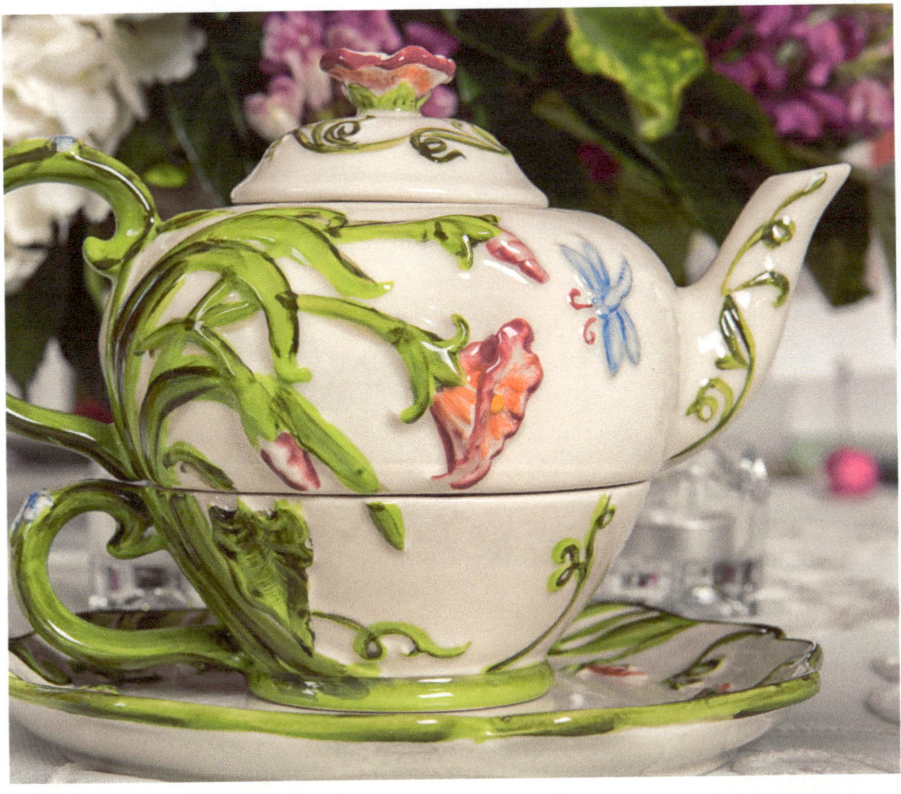

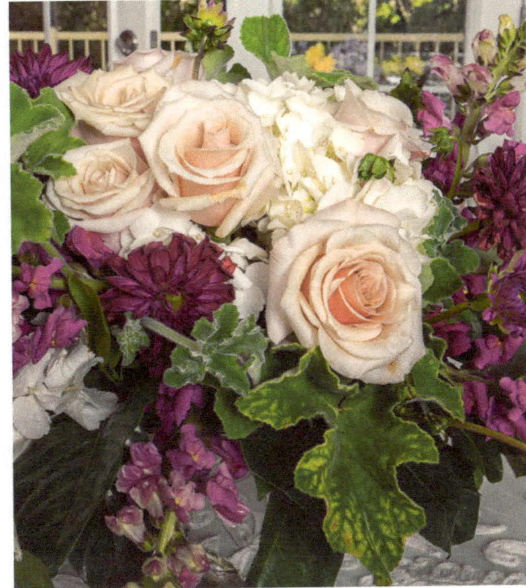

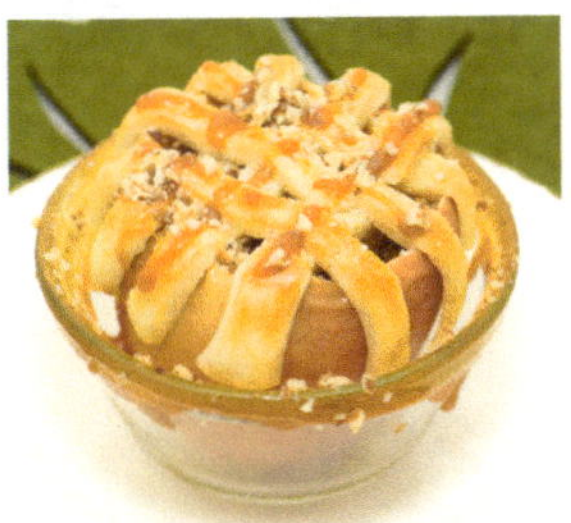

Baked Apple Cup

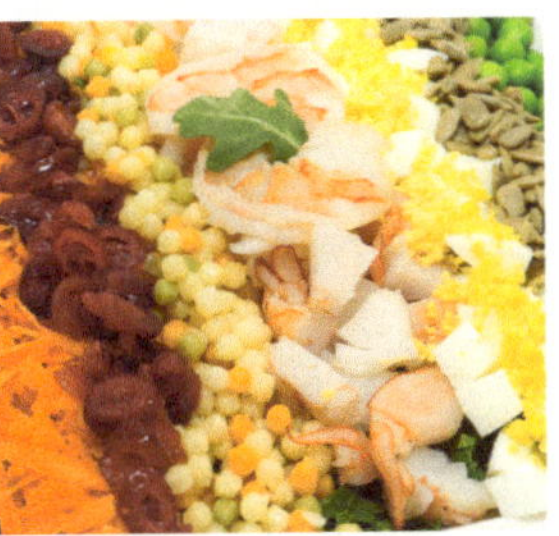

Poached Shrimp Chop Salad

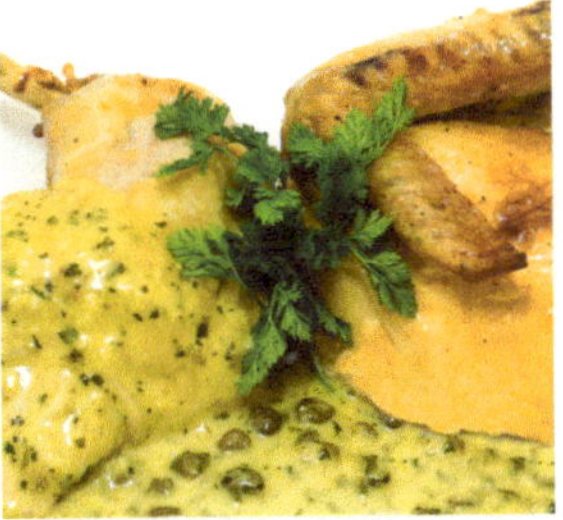

Lemon Roasted Chicken

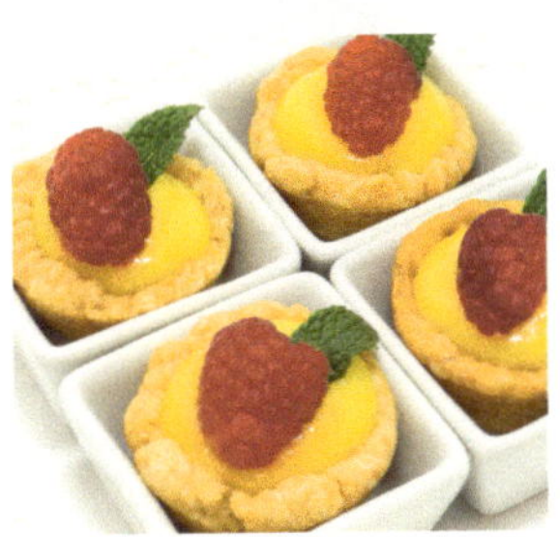

Lemon Tarts

Course highlights:

À la Carte Menu

Amuse-bouche
Orange Cranberry and Apricot Scones | Devonshire Cream
Baked Apple Cup
COCKTAIL PAIRING: *Mini Watermelon Sorbet Shooter
with Mint*

First Course: Appetizer
Sweet Crepes | An Assortment of Fruit Purees
Poached Shrimp Chop Salad | Lemon Herb Vinaigrette
WINE PAIRING: *Conundrum White*

Second Course: Entrée
Honey Glazed Rainbow Carrots
Chicken & Green Cauliflower Frittata
Mini Croquet Mousier Sandwiches | Pico de Gallo
Creamy Three Cheese Risotto | Sweet Peas
Lemon Roasted Chicken | Béarnaise Sauce | Capers
Seared Ahi Tuna | Grand Mariner Buerre Blanc Sauce
Top Sirloin Roast | Chimichurri Sauce
Horseradish Crème Fraiche
WINE PAIRING: *Le Canon De Cote Montpezat Rosé*

Third Course: Dessert
Tea Cakes | Chantilly Whipped Cream
Lemon Tarts | Fresh Raspberries
WINE PAIRING: *Mauro Sebaste Moscato d'Asti*
ASSORTMENT OF TEAS AND COFFEE

Dining Service Style: *Buffet Service with Server Assistance*
Amuse-bouche is served at the table. First, Second, and
Third Course are arranged on serving tables. Guests will
serve themselves from the buffet tables. When their plates
are filled, guests take them to the dining table to enjoy. If
assistance is needed, servers should attend to the guests.
Servers will provide beverage service at tableside.

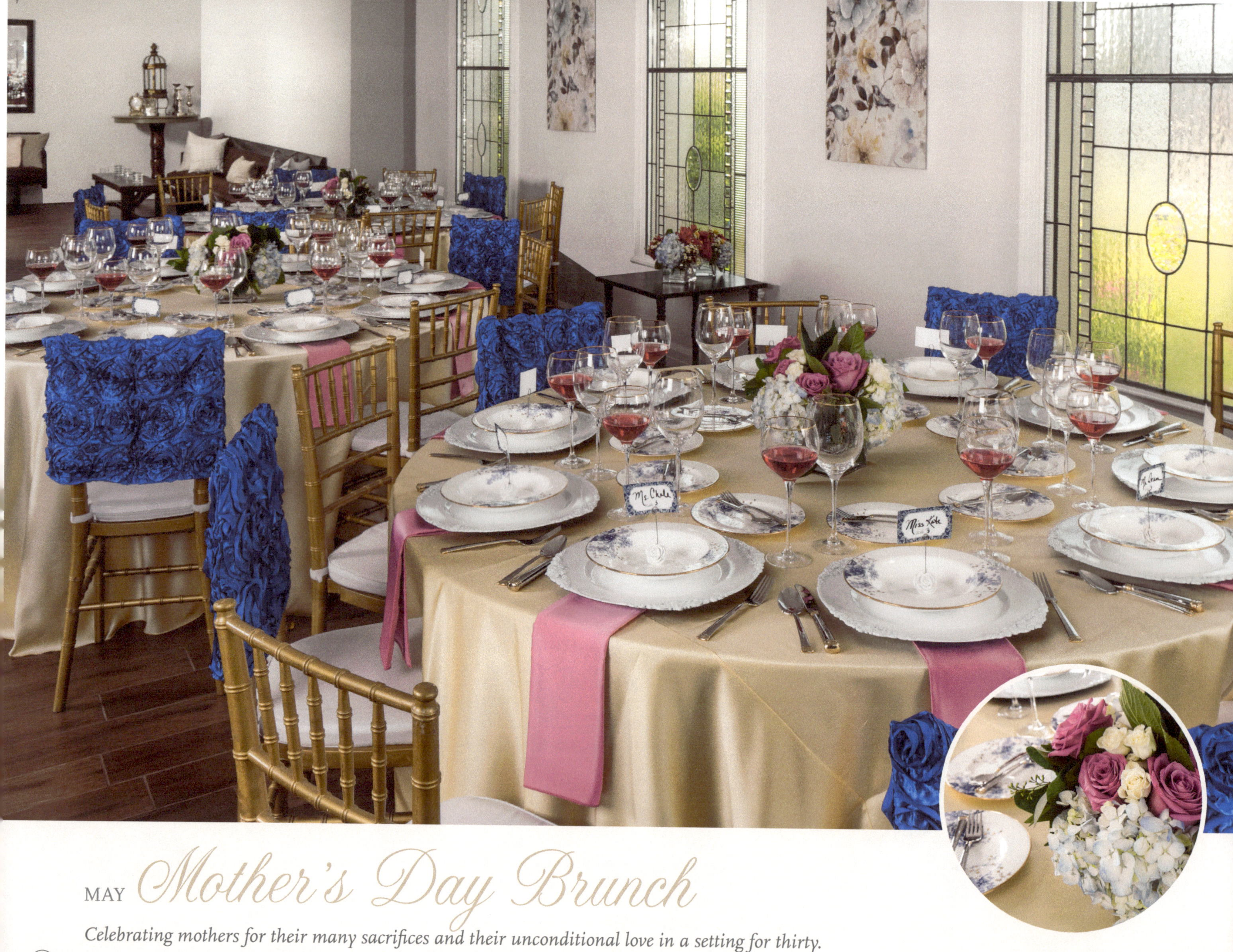

MAY *Mother's Day Brunch*

Celebrating mothers for their many sacrifices and their unconditional love in a setting for thirty.

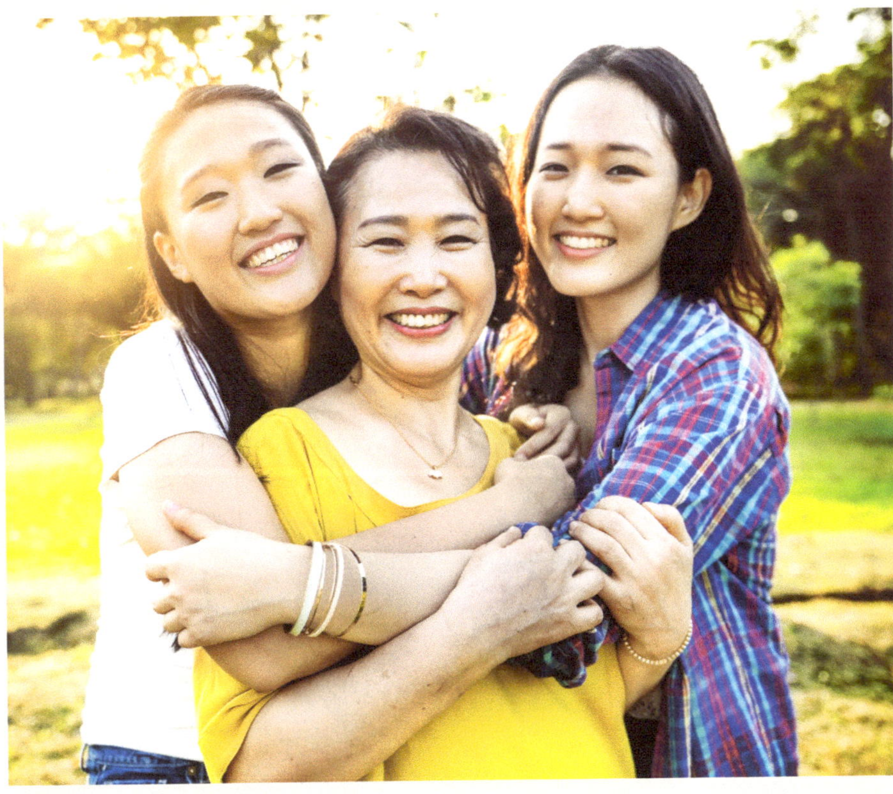

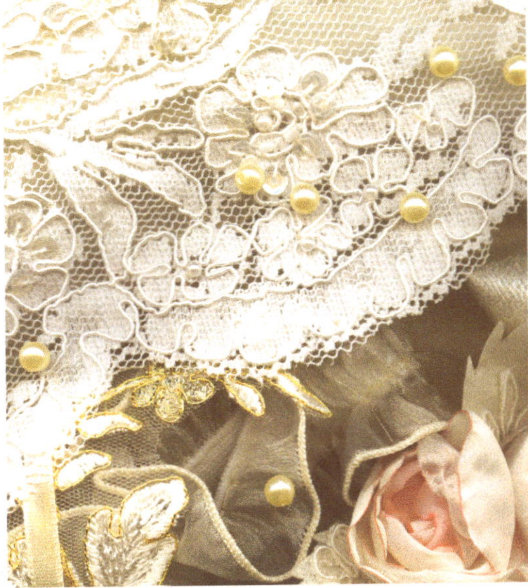

À la Carte Menu

Amuse-bouche
Herb-Crusted Goat Cheese | Dried Fruits
Honey Butter Crostini
  COCKTAIL PAIRING: *Mimosa*

First Course: Appetizer
Fried Green Tomatoes | Lemon Garlic Crème Fraiche
Zucchini Gazpacho | Lump Snow Crab
Sweet Bell Peppers
  WINE PAIRING: *Sanrocchetto Verdicchio Jesi White Wine*

Second Course: Entrée
Rosemary Buttermilk Drop Biscuits | Sausage Gravy
French Toast | Chantilly Whip Cream
Maple Blueberry Sausage | Poached Eggs | Maltaise Sauce
Baby Bok Choy | Roasted Garlic | Sesame Seeds
Rhubarb Mashed Potatoes | Fennel
Zucchini Ribbons and Eggplant | Dijon Mustard Vinaigrette
Sweet and Sour Pork Tenderloin | Teriyaki Sauce
Red Grouper Poelé | Fruit Salsa
  WINE PAIRING: *Sobon Estate Viognier White Wine*

Third Course: Dessert
Mango Sorbet | Fresh Fruit
Apple Parfait | Whipped Mascarpone Cheese
  WINE PAIRING: *Terre Rouge Muscat Petits Grains*
  ASSORTMENT OF TEAS AND COFFEE

Dining Service Style: *Buffet Service with Server Assistance*
Amuse-bouche is served at the table. First, Second, and
Third Course are arranged on serving tables. Guests will
serve themselves from the buffet tables. When their plates
are filled, guests take them to the dining table to enjoy. If
assistance is needed, servers should attend to the guests.
Servers will provide beverage service at tableside.

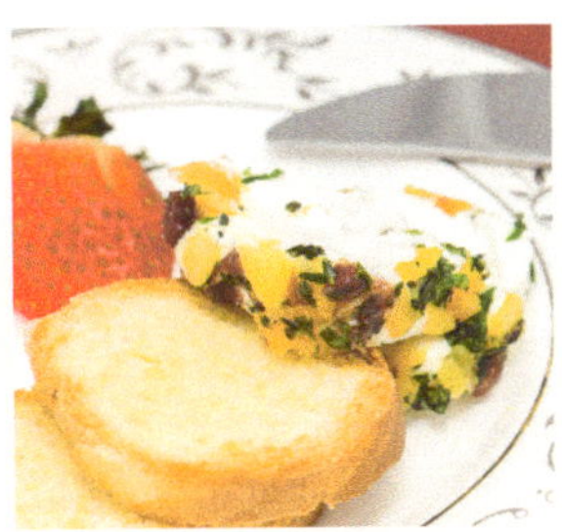

Herb-Crusted Goat Cheese

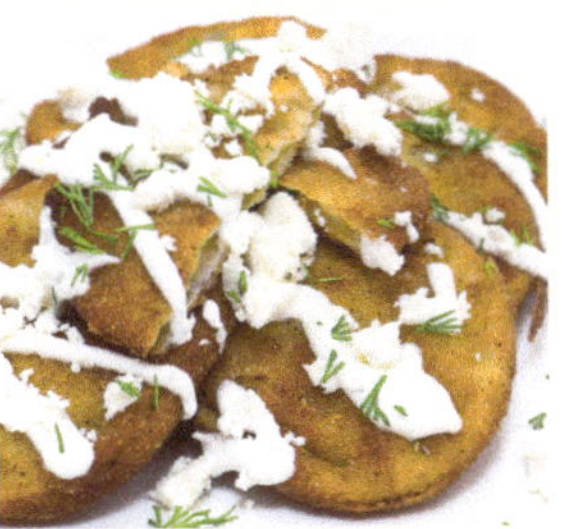

Fried Green Tomatoes

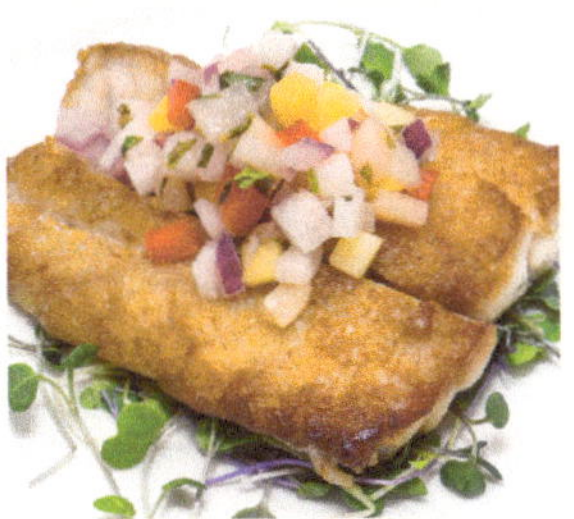

Red Grouper Poelé

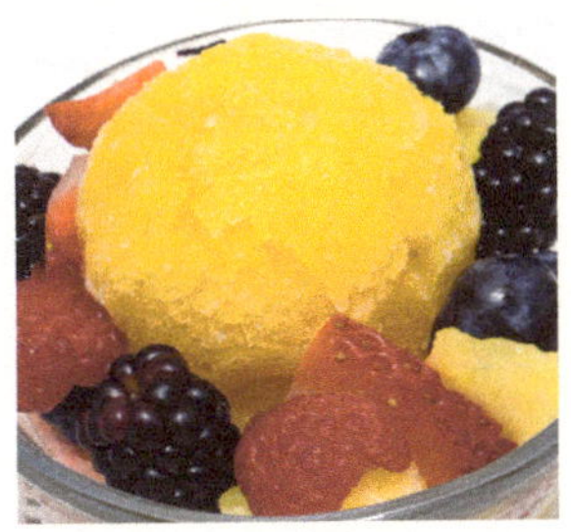

Mango Sorbet

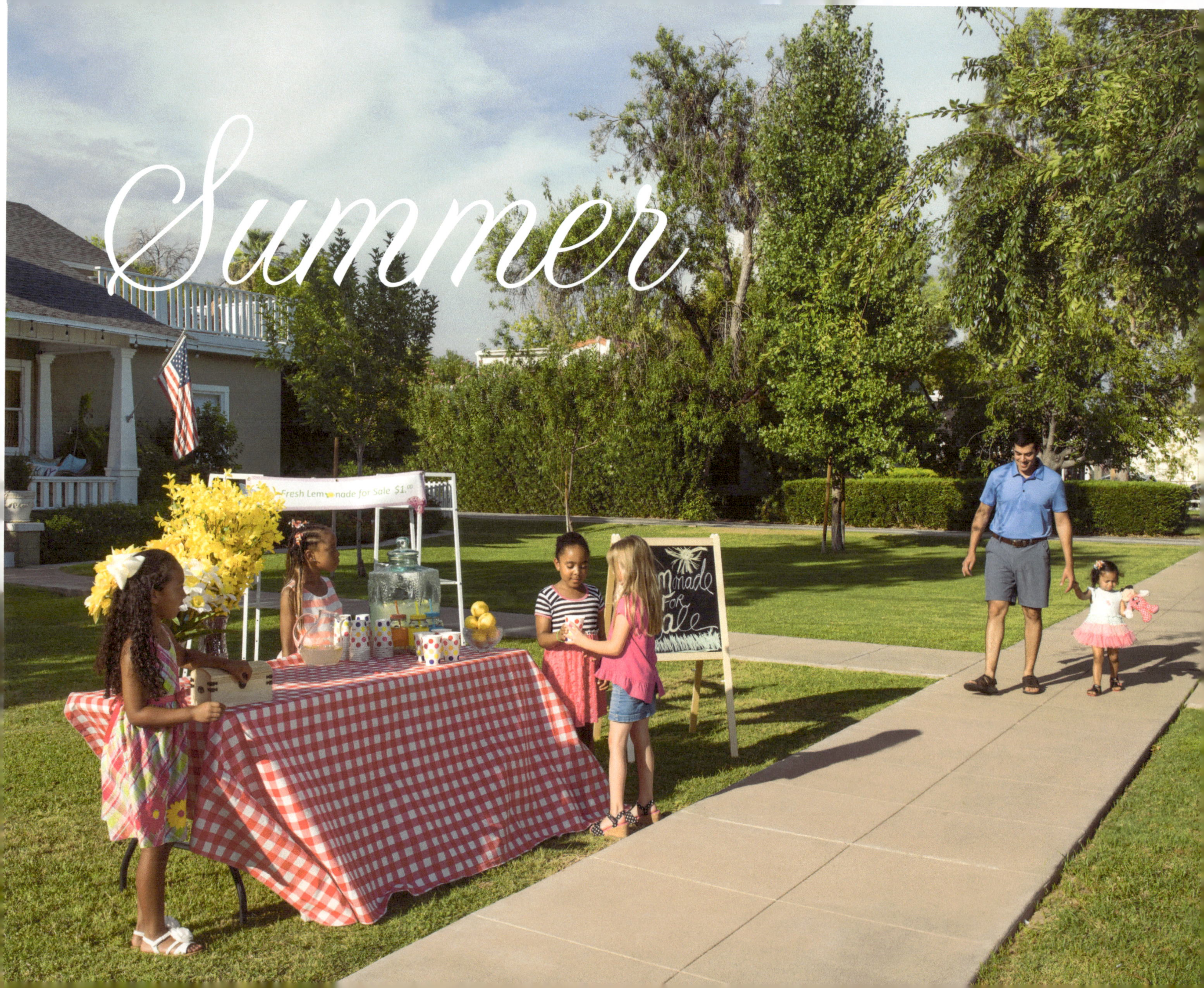
Summer
Fresh Lemonade for Sale $1.00

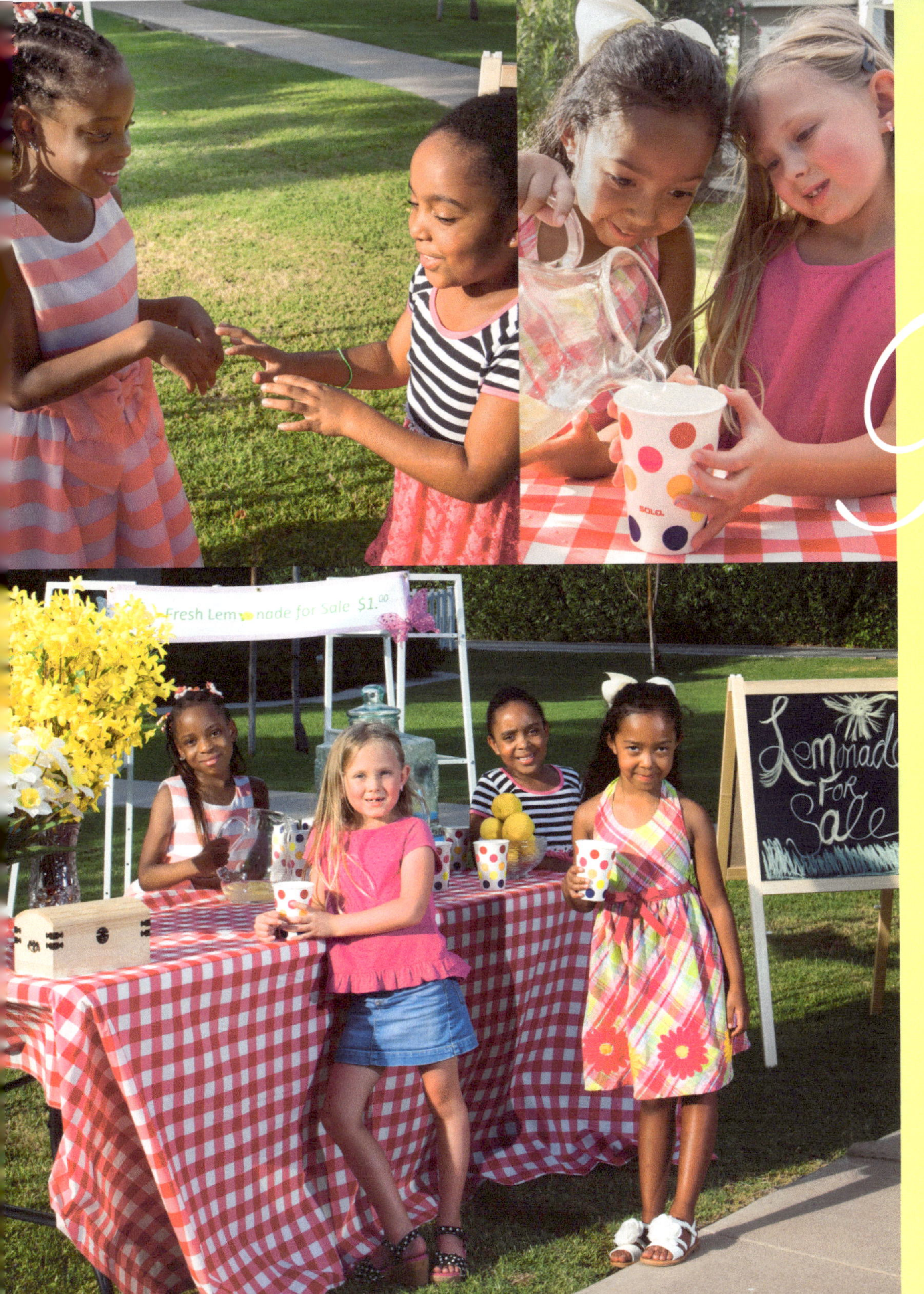

The long days of summer come with a gentle breeze, and nature is in full bloom. There is enough quiet time to dream and wonder about the beauty of life. Romance is also in the air. It's a time when couples wed and then honeymoon in exotic locations. Summer reminds me of outdoor cooking, picnics, and summer salads. Hamburgers and hotdogs cooked on an open grill at the beach while playing volleyball or baseball under the hot sun. Laughter, fun, carnivals, firework shows, and planned vacations, all while relaxing with loved ones.

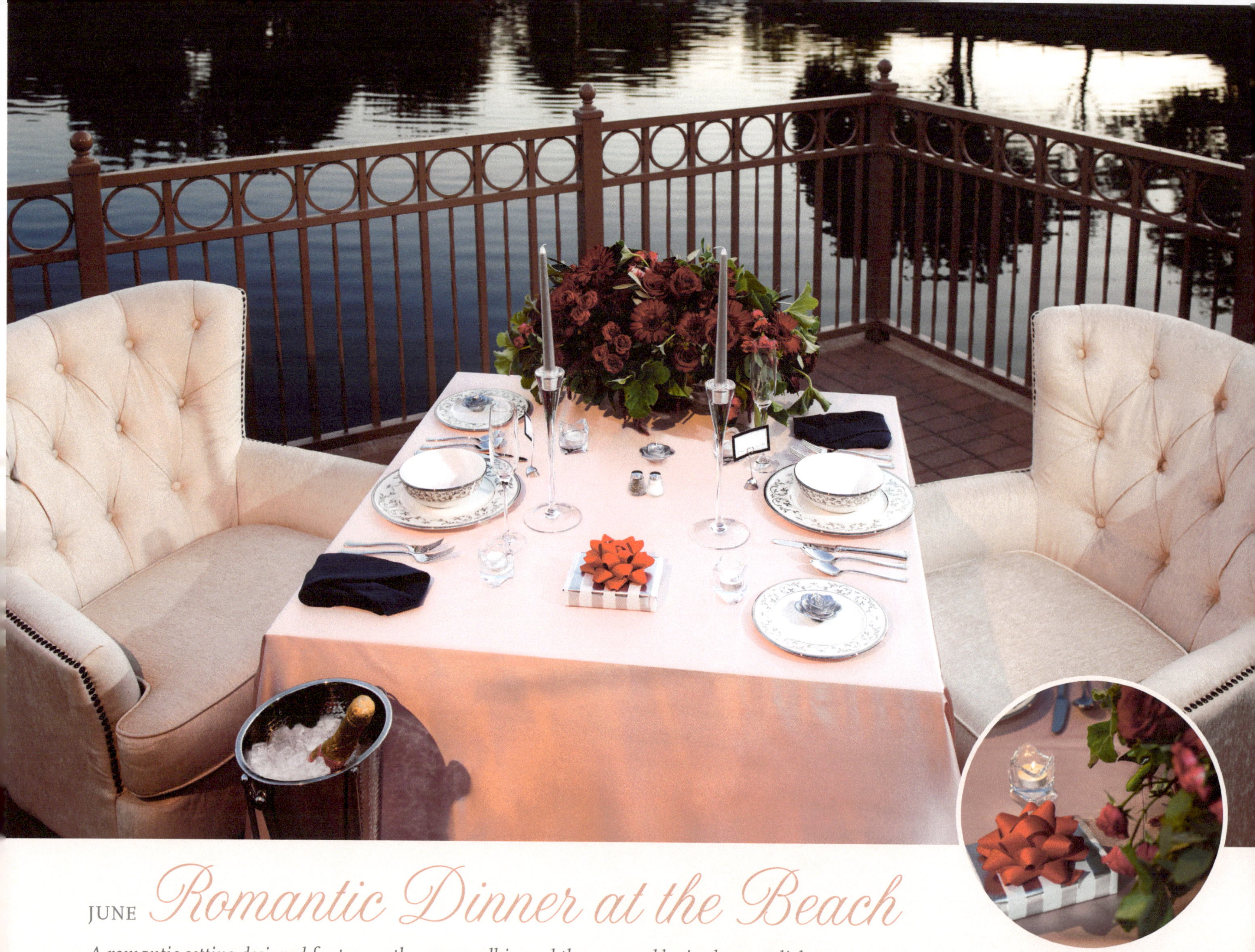

Romantic Dinner at the Beach

A romantic setting designed for two as the waves roll in and the sea sparkles in the moonlight.

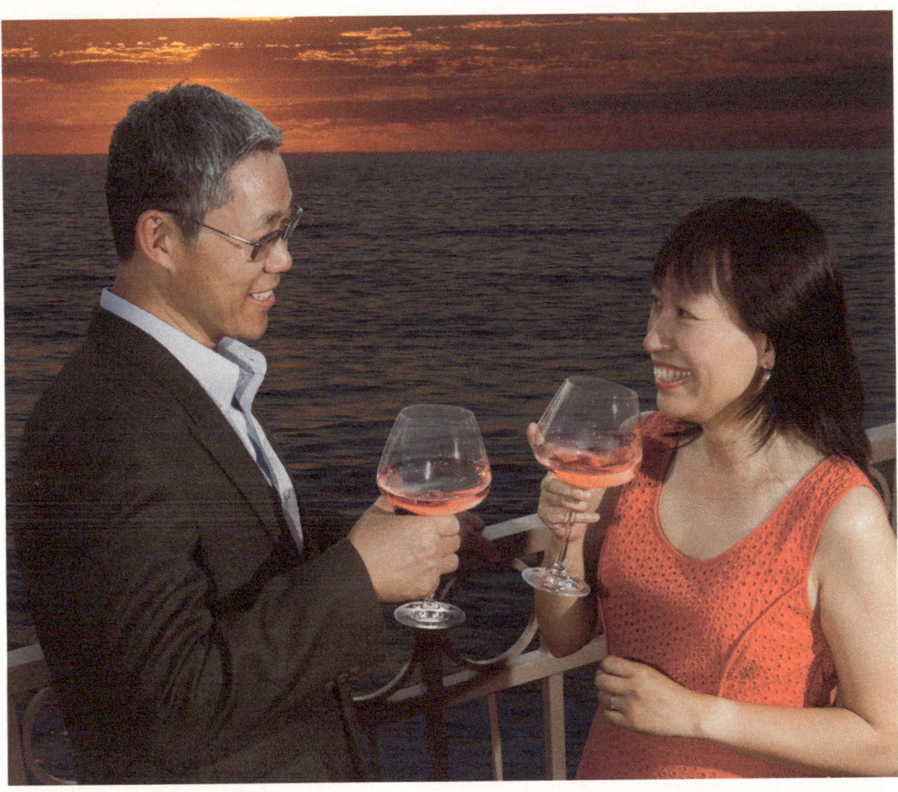

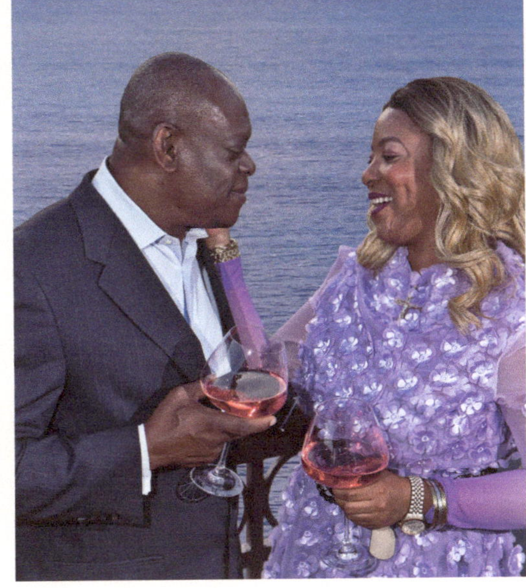

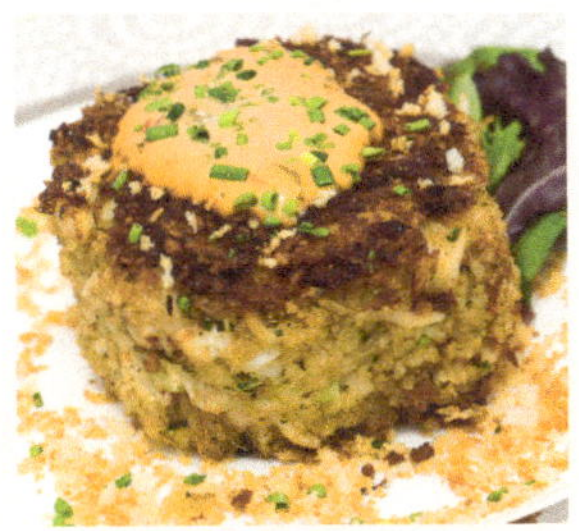

Crab Cake

À la Carte Menu

Amuse-bouche
Crab Cake | Spicy Remoulade Sauce
  COCKTAIL PAIRING: *Vara Garnacha Rosado Rioja DOC,*
  New Mexico

First Course: Appetizer
Alexandria Consommé Soup | Vegetables
Chicken Quenelles
Steamed Mussels | Pearled Couscous | Cream Sauce
  WINE PAIRING: *Patz & Hall Chardonnay Dutton Ranch*

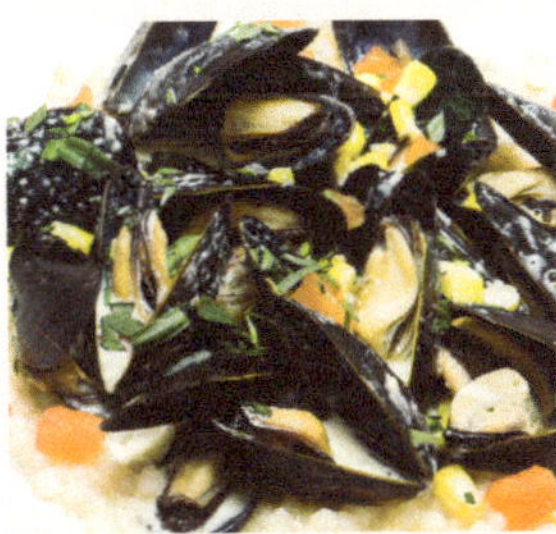

Steamed Mussels

Second Course: Entrée
Sliced Purple Potatoes | Compound Butter
Sautéed Brussel Sprouts | Crispy Bacon | Fennel
Stuffed Sole | Salmon Mousse | Lemon Aioli
Fried Lobster Roll | Béarnaise Butter | Black Truffle Oil
  WINE PAIRING: *Champagne Mailly Grand Cru*
  "O" de Mailly

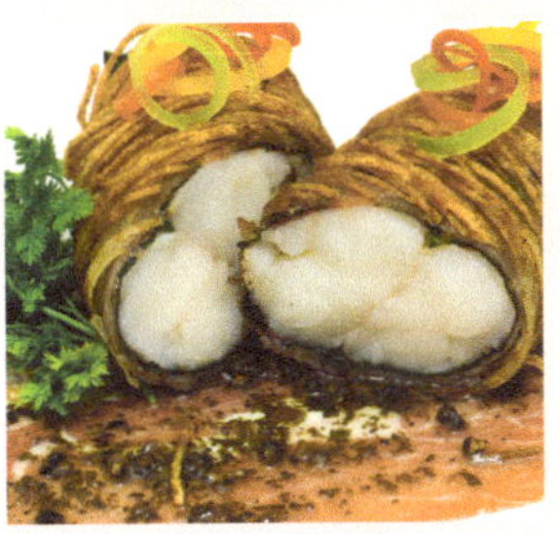

Fried Lobster Roll

Third Course: Dessert
Passion Fruit Mousse | Raspberry Coulis
  WINE PAIRING: *Inniskillin Ice Wine Cabernet Franc*
  ASSORTMENT OF TEAS AND COFFEE

Dining Service Style: *Formal Plated Service*
Guests are seated. Each course will be prepared and
portioned in the kitchen, arranged on china, and served by
servers to the guests. Beverage service will be completed
at tableside by the servers unless there is a designated bar
station. In this instance, the server will obtain a beverage
order, fulfill the order, and serve the beverage to the guests
tableside.

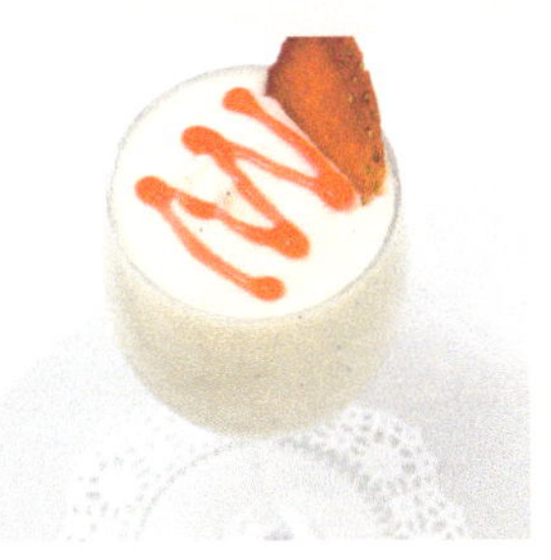

Passion Fruit Mousse

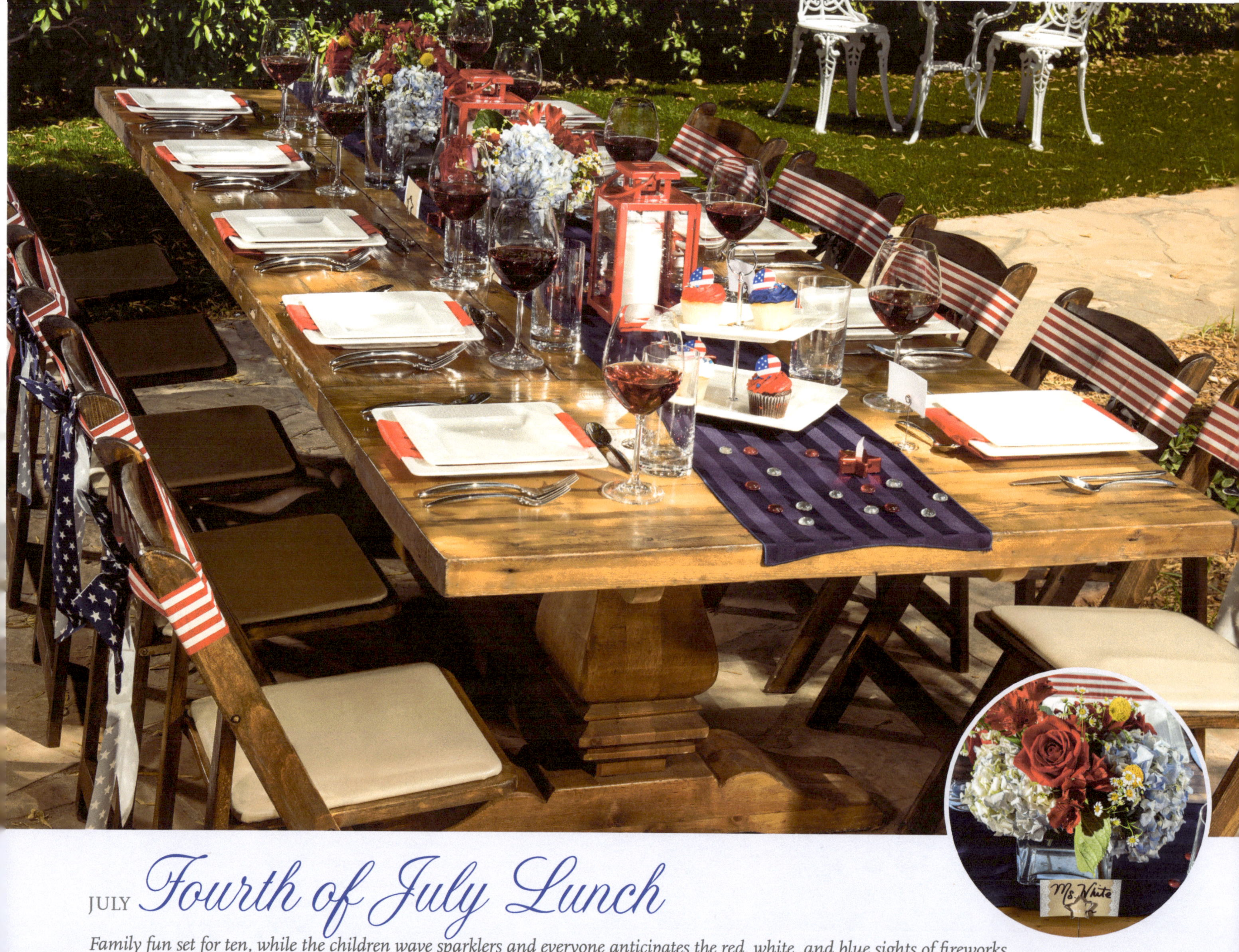

JULY *Fourth of July Lunch*

Family fun set for ten, while the children wave sparklers and everyone anticipates the red, white, and blue sights of fireworks.

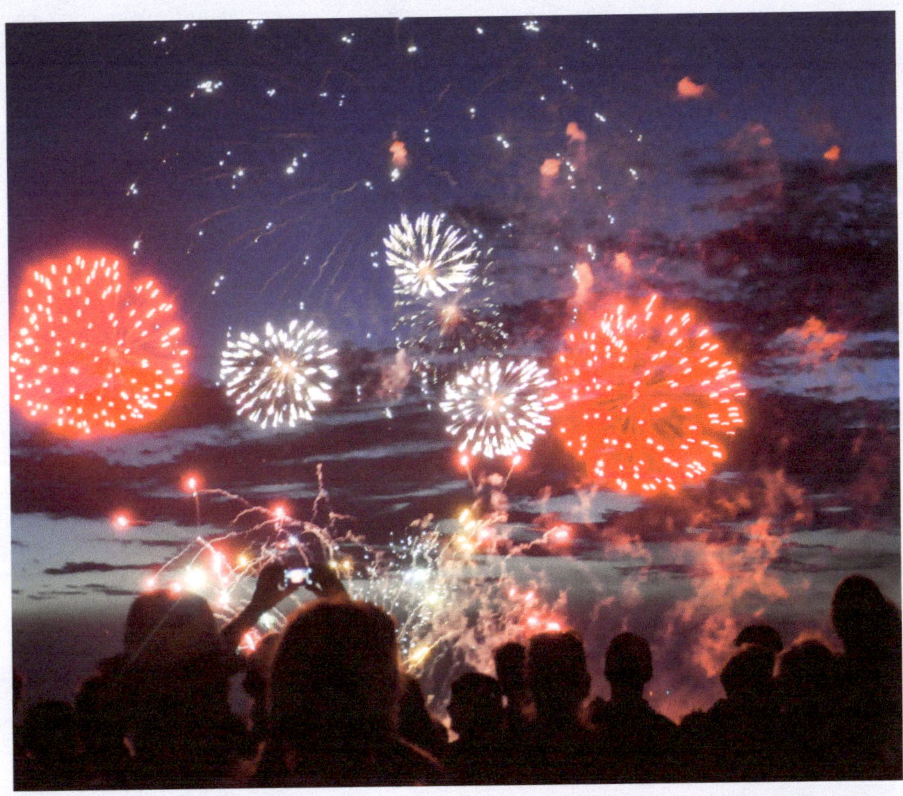

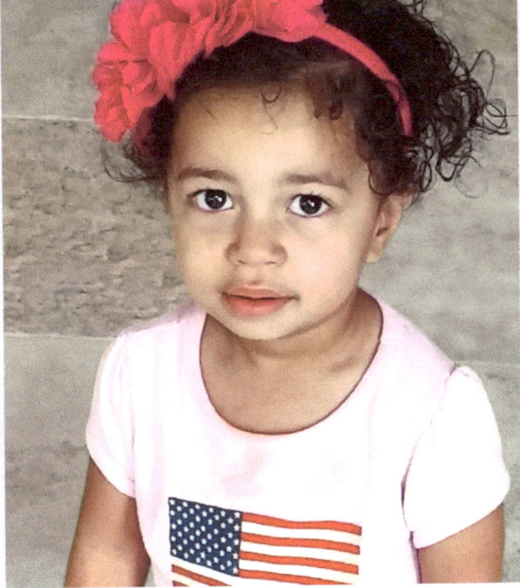

Course highlights:

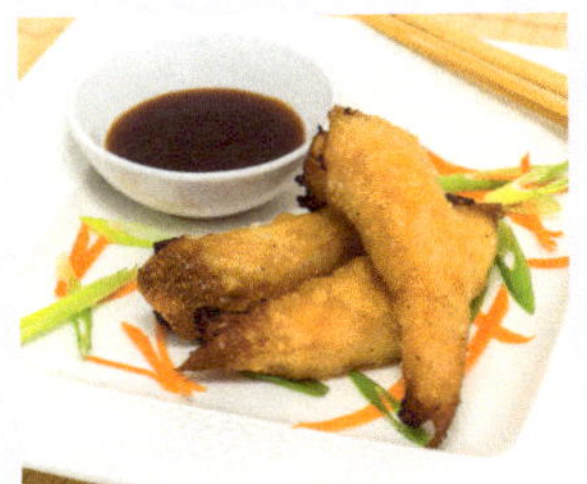

Firecracker Shrimp

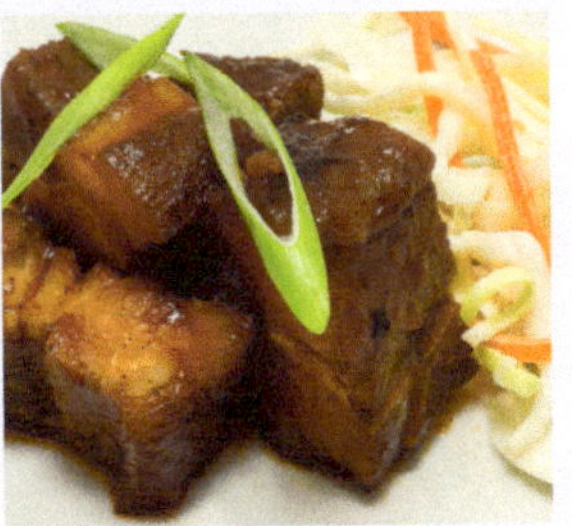

Braised Pork Belly

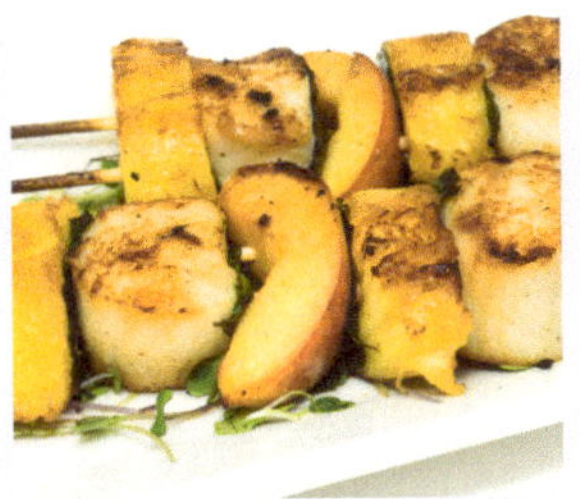

Pan Seared Sea Scallops

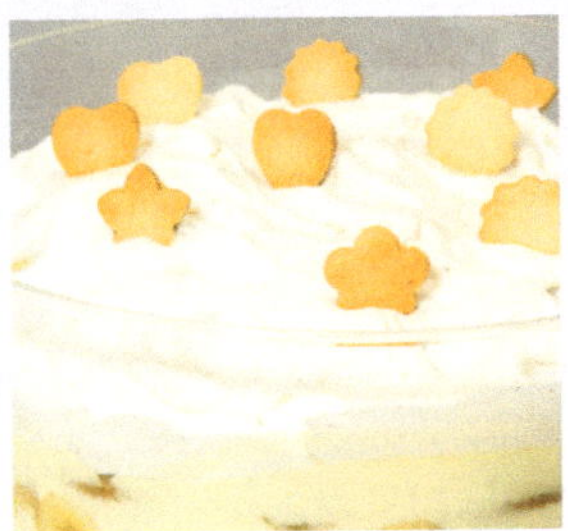

Banana Pudding

À la Carte Menu

Amuse-bouche
Firecracker Shrimp | Asian Sauce
  COCKTAIL PAIRING: *Margaritas*

First Course: Appetizer
Strawberry Salad | Goat Cheese Croutons
Braised Pork Belly | Spicy Asian BBQ Sauce | Cole Slaw
  WINE PAIRING: *Hugues Beauvignac Picpoul White Wine*

Second Course: Entrée
Potato Salad | Sliced Hard-Boiled Egg | Paprika
Baked Beans | Crispy Pancetta
Wild and Brown Rice Medley | Baby Corn | Dried Fruit
Tri-colored Asparagus | Balsamic Vinegar
Grilled Chicken Satay | Teriyaki Sauce
Grilled Spicy Pork Kebabs | Green Chilies | Cilantro
Grilled Lamb Kebabs | Sweet Onion | Red Peppers
Pan Seared Sea Scallops | Peaches | Pineapple
  WINE PAIRING: *Sobon Rezerve Zinfandel*

Third Course: Dessert
Banana Pudding | Vanilla Shortbread Cookies
Peach Buckle Cake | Lemon Hazelnut Ice Cream
  WINE PAIRING: *Offley 10 Year Tawny Port*
  ASSORTMENT OF TEAS AND COFFEE

Dining Service Style: *Family Style Service with Server Assistance*
Guests are seated. Large serving platters and bowls are filled with foods in the kitchen and set on the dining tables by servers. Guests help themselves as they pass the foods to each other. Beverages are served to the guests tableside.

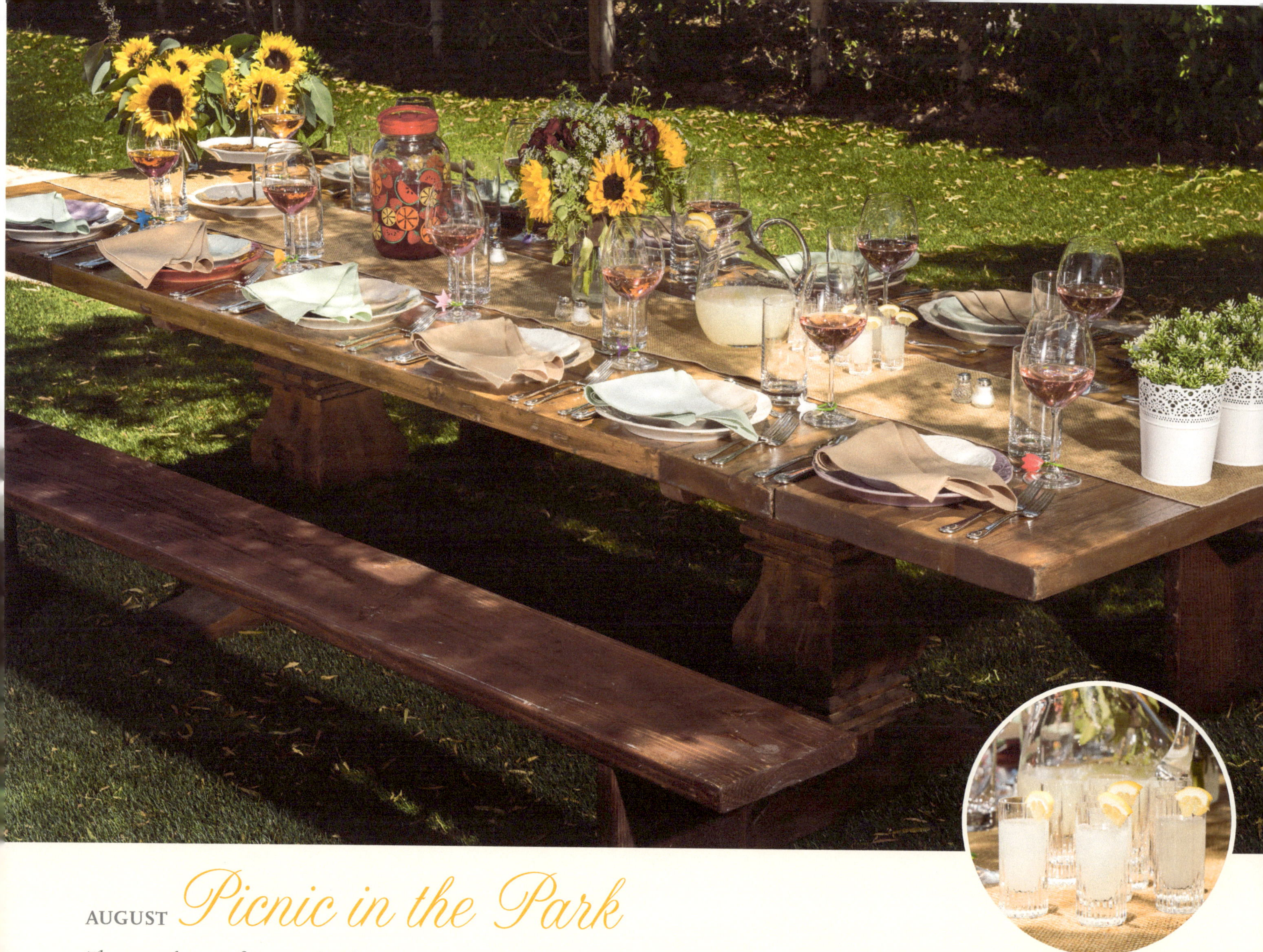

 Picnic in the Park

The warm breeze of summer brushes your skin and cool green grass tickles your feet at a family picnic set for twelve.

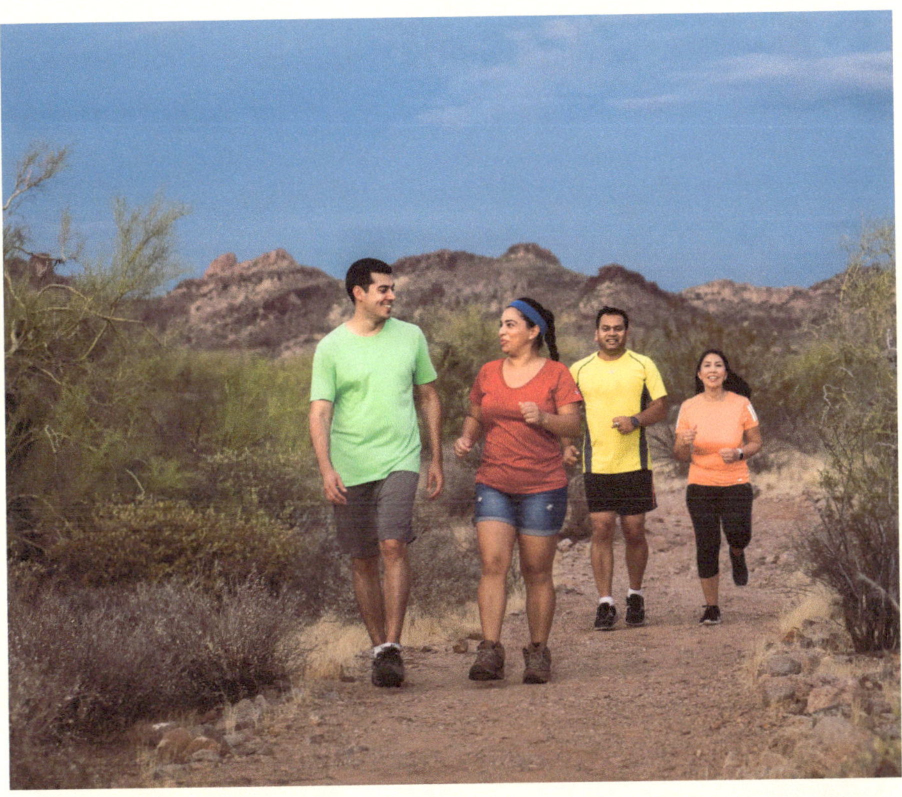

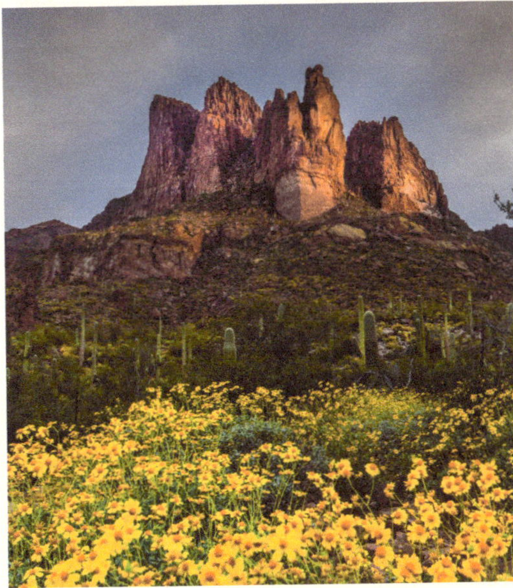

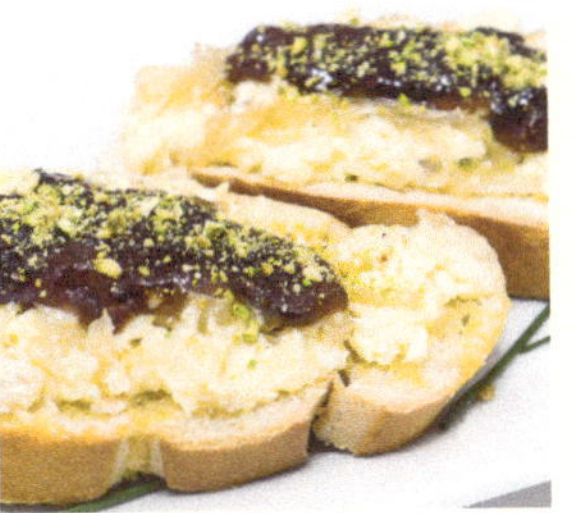

Roasted Brie Bruschetta

À la Carte Menu

Amuse-bouche
Roasted Brie Bruschetta | Pistachios | Black Fig Compote
COCKTAIL PAIRING: *Mojitos*

First Course: Appetizer
Summer Watermelon Salad | Balsamic Glaze Dressing
Smoked Brisket Sliders | White Truffle Popcorn
WINE PAIRING: *Framingham Marlborough Sauvignon Blanc*

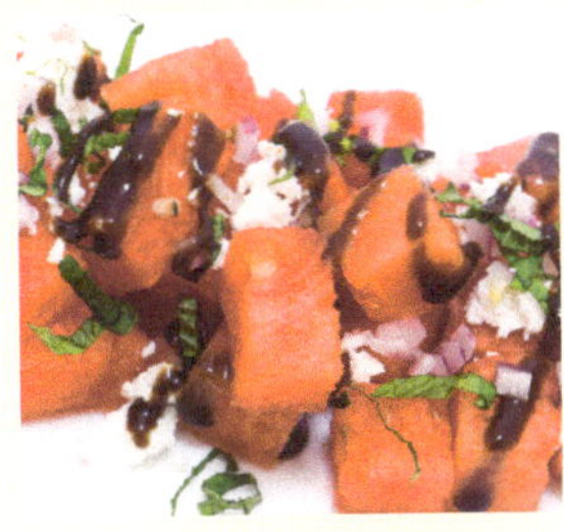

Summer Watermelon Salad

Second Course: Entrée
Golden French Fries | Cotija Cheese | Parsley
Okra Succotash
Antipasto Charcuterie Board
Fried Buttermilk Chicken
Baked Halibut Fish Stick | Zesty Tartar Sauce
WINE PAIRING: *Clos St Michel Chateauneuf-du-Pape Blanc*

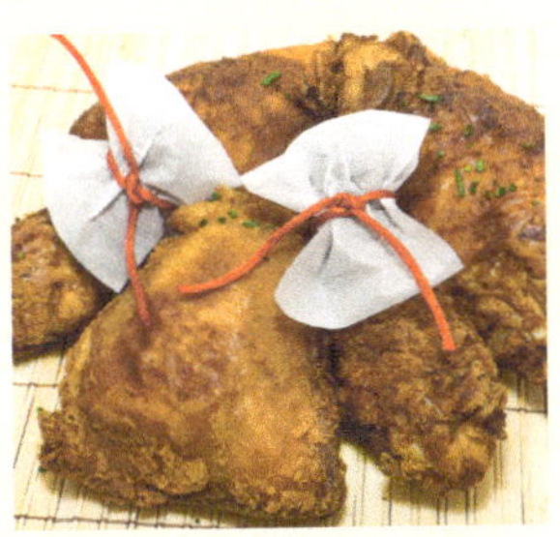

Fried Buttermilk Chicken

Third Course: Dessert
Mini Fruit Tart | Caramel Bird's Nest
WINE PAIRING: *Bridgman Riesling*
ASSORTMENT OF TEAS AND COFFEE

Dining Service Style: *Family Style Service with Server Assistance*
Guests are seated. Large serving platters and bowls are filled with foods in the kitchen and set on the dining tables by servers. Guests help themselves as they pass the foods to each other. Beverages are served to the guests tableside.

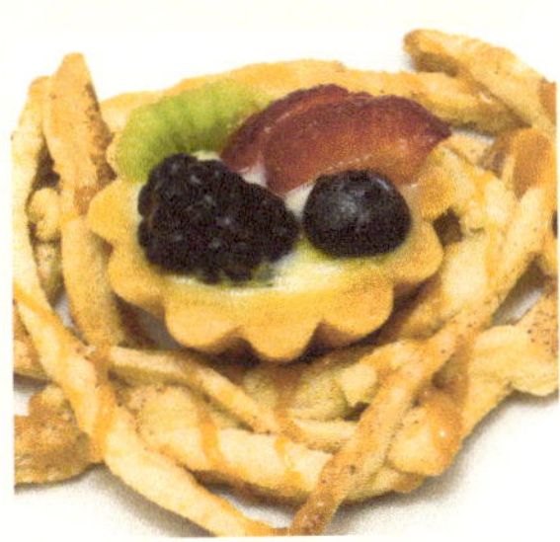

Mini Fruit Tart

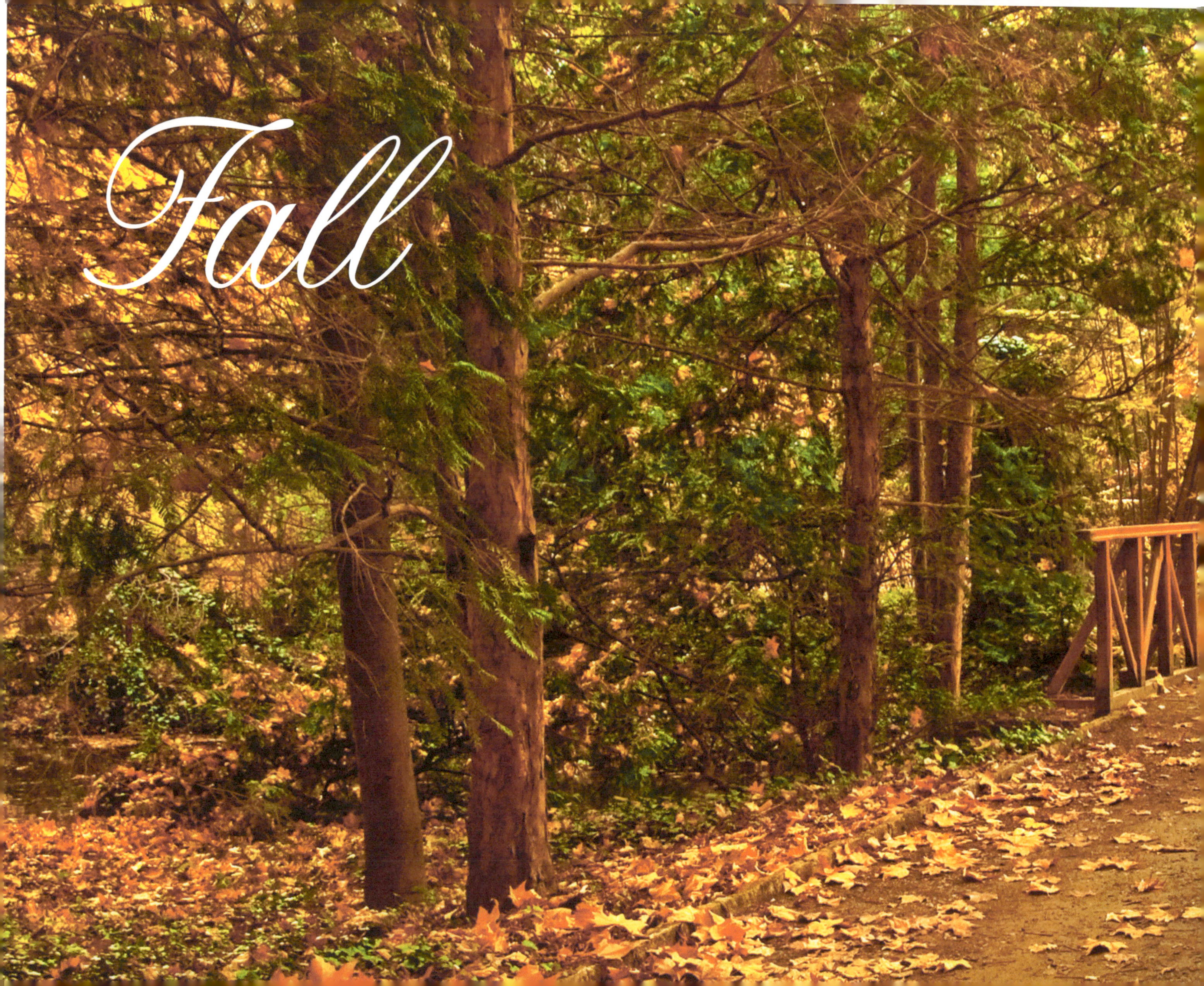
Fall

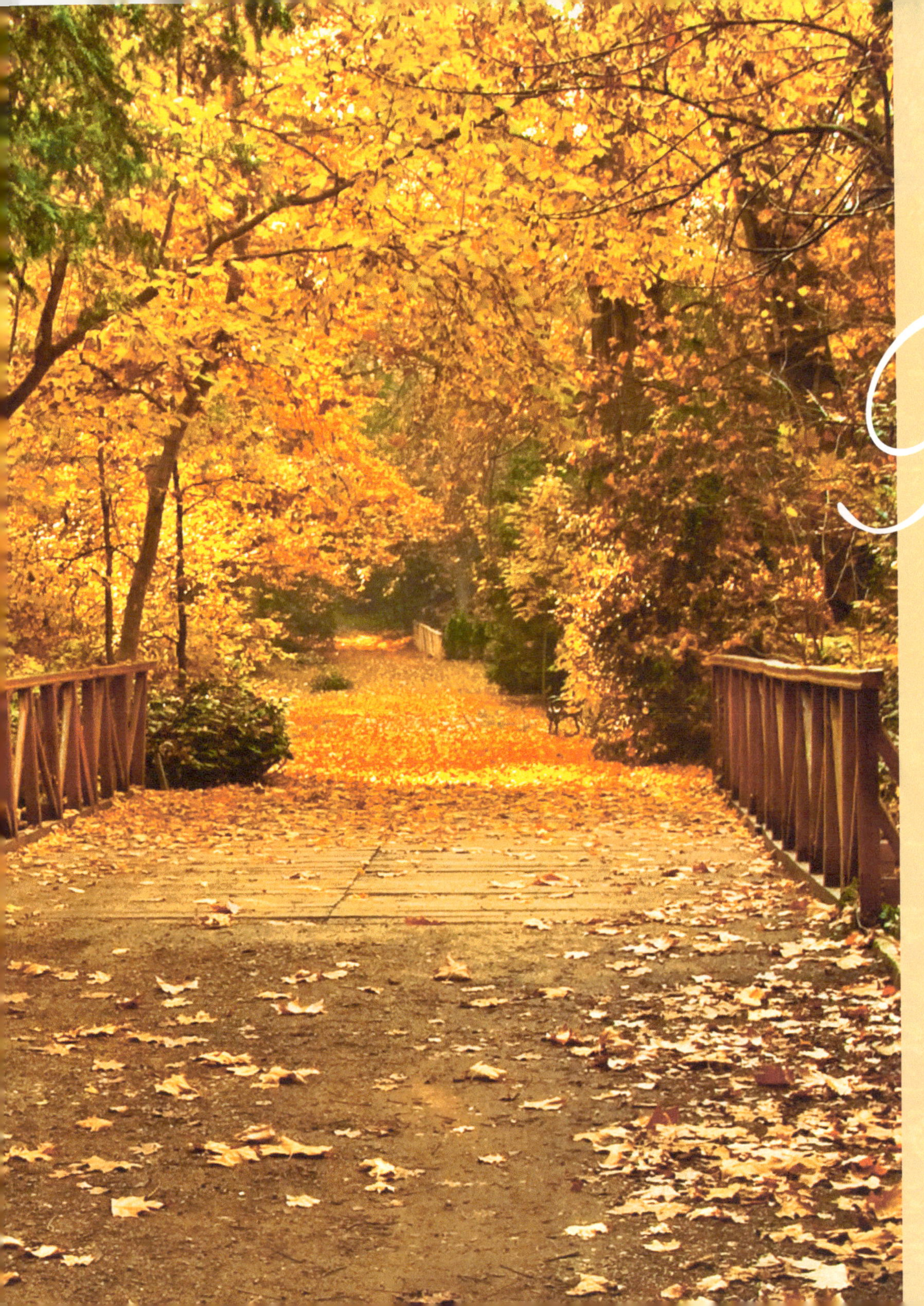

The smells of comfort foods sing a symphony of cinnamon, nutmeg, vanilla, and cloves. Baked apples, pecans, and walnuts alongside warming soups, stews, and pies. A time of outdoor fun: children playing in the falling leaves, ladies drinking hot chocolate with marshmallows, and dads and sons playing tag football in the backyard. Strolls with family and friends, over bridges, among trees turning rich colors of red, yellow, orange, brown, and purple. Everyone enjoys the last days of warmth before the cold winds of winter arrive.

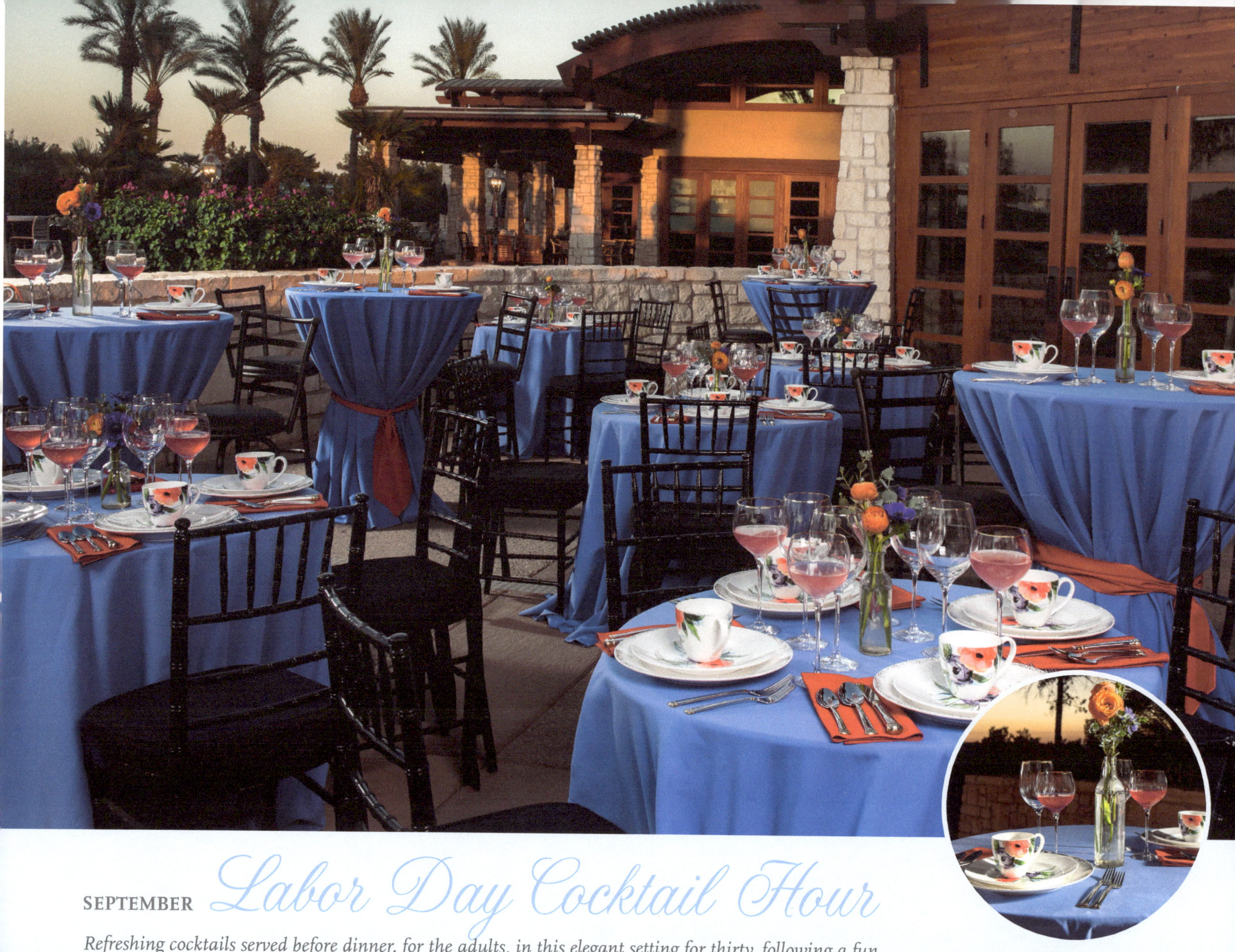

Labor Day Cocktail Hour

Refreshing cocktails served before dinner, for the adults, in this elegant setting for thirty, following a fun game of family softball.

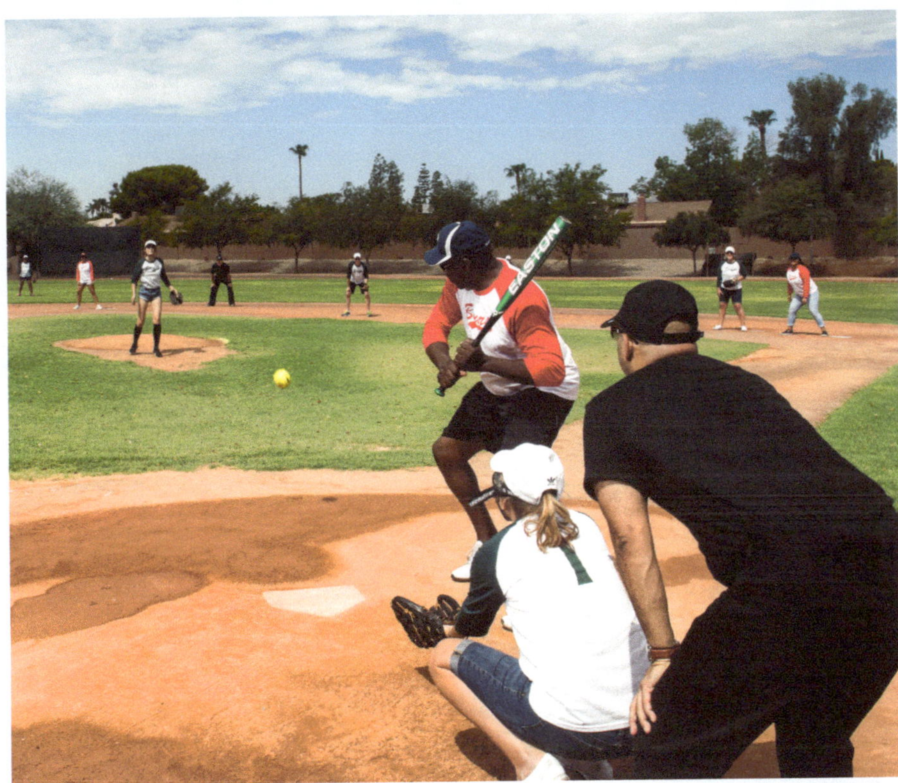

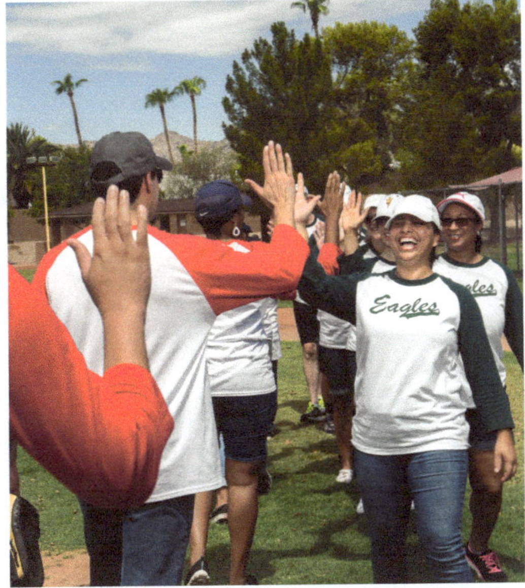

À la Carte Menu

Amuse-bouche

Bacon-Wrapped Sirloin | Bacon-Wrapped Chicken
   COCKTAIL PAIRING: *Manhattan*

First Course: Appetizer

Red and Yellow Beet Salad | Gorgonzola Cheese
Napa Cabbage
   WINE PAIRING: *Domaine Chenevieres*
         Chablis Les Grandes Vignes

Second Course: Entrée

Buttermilk Cheese Rolls
String Potatoes | Julienne Jalapenos
Warm Cabbage | Crispy Prosciutto
Sautéed Baby Corn and Carrots
Pulled Pork Tacos | Cilantro-Lime Slaw
Chicken Salad Sandwich | Baby Arugula
Grilled Lamb Chops | Mint Yogurt Sauce
   WINE PAIRING: *Belle Glos Pinot Noir Clark & Telephone*

Third Course: Dessert

Bourbon Bread Pudding | Caramel Sauce
   CORDIAL PAIRING: *Bailey's Irish Cream*
   ASSORTMENT OF TEAS AND COFFEE

Dining Service Style: *Action Stations with Plated Entrées*
Action stations are similar to a buffet dining service. With buffet dining service, guests serve themselves from buffet tables and take their filled plates to the dining table to enjoy. An action station dining service utilizes a culinary specialist at each station to assist with the plating of entrées for the guests. The cuisines are plated on china at the buffet table, typically in advance of guests arriving or served at the time of request. Guests will select their cuisines and take their plated entrée of choice to their seats. Servers will assist as needed and beverage service is completed tableside.

Course highlights:

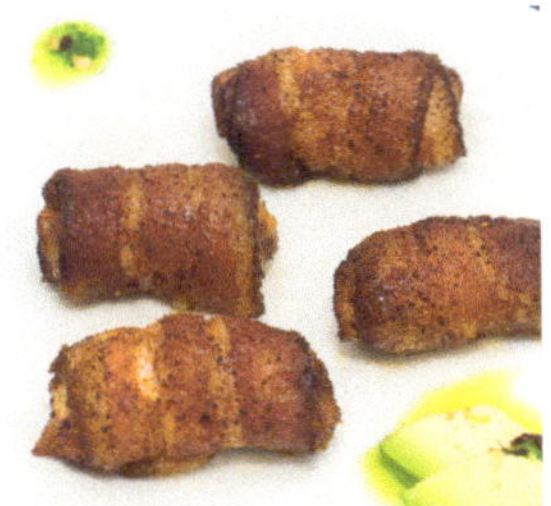

Bacon-Wrapped Chicken

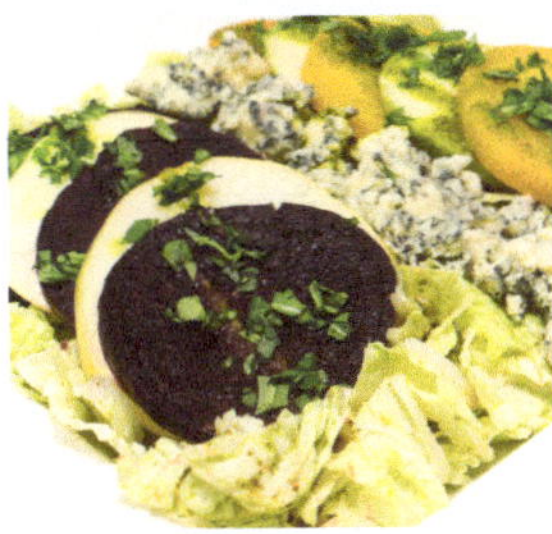

Red and Yellow Beet Salad

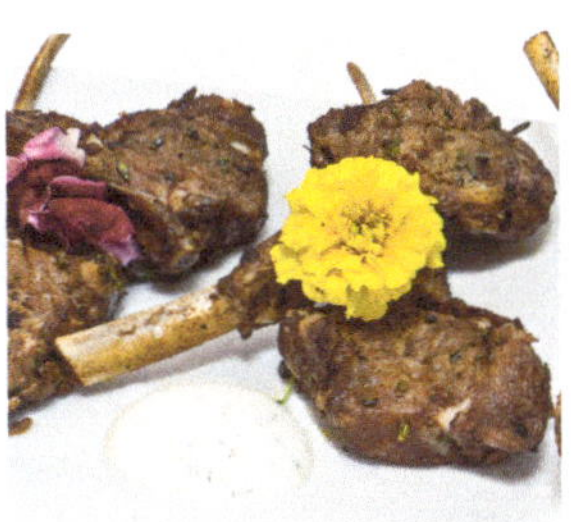

Grilled Lamb Chops

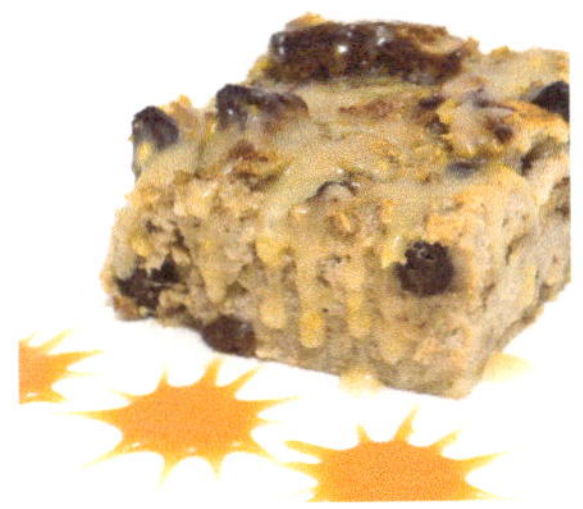

Bourbon Bread Pudding

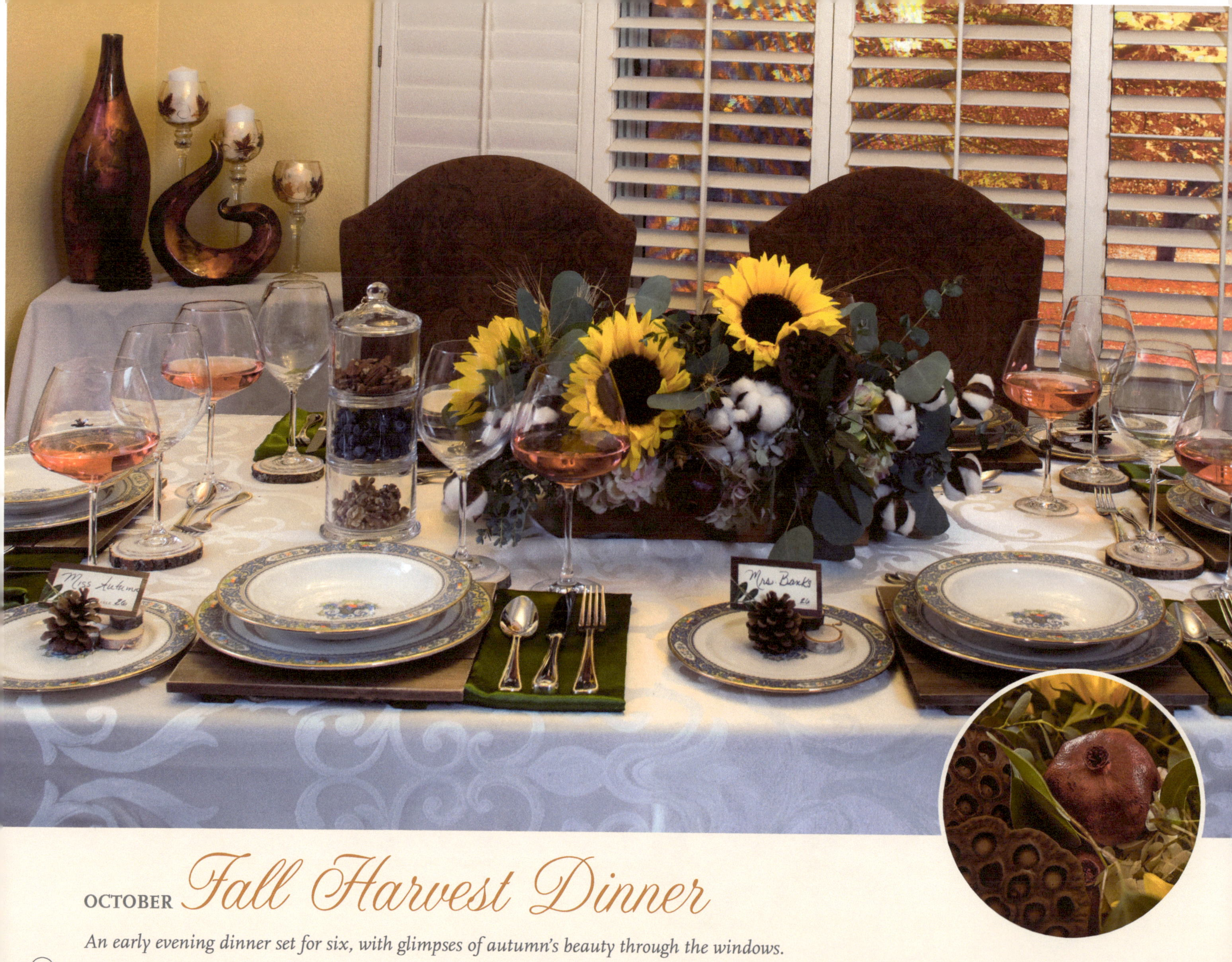

OCTOBER *Fall Harvest Dinner*

An early evening dinner set for six, with glimpses of autumn's beauty through the windows.

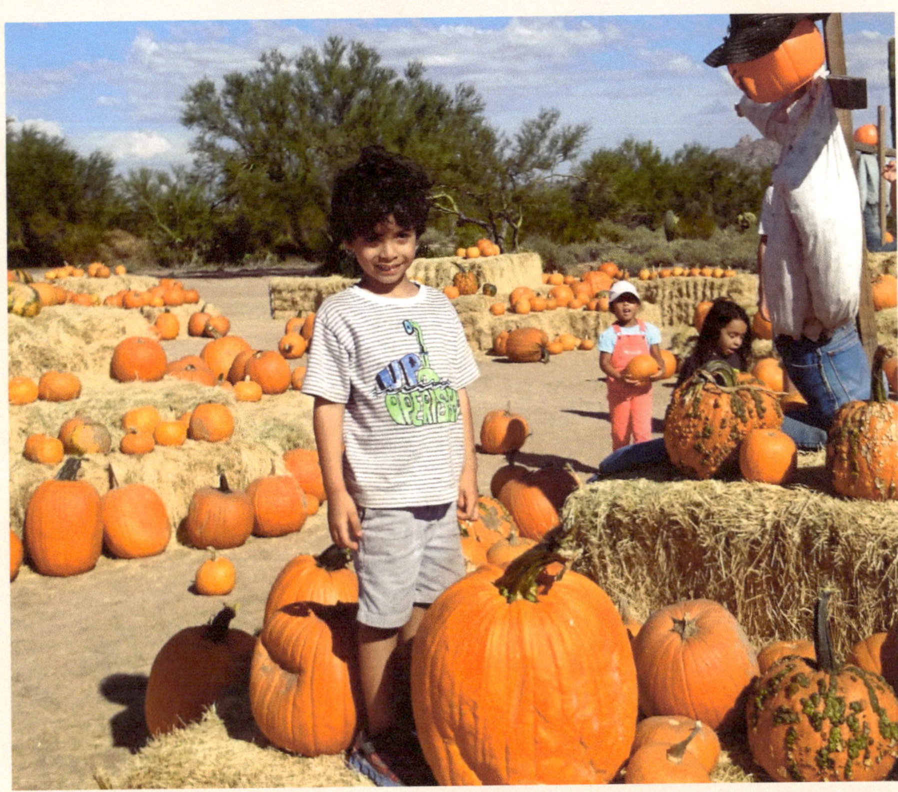

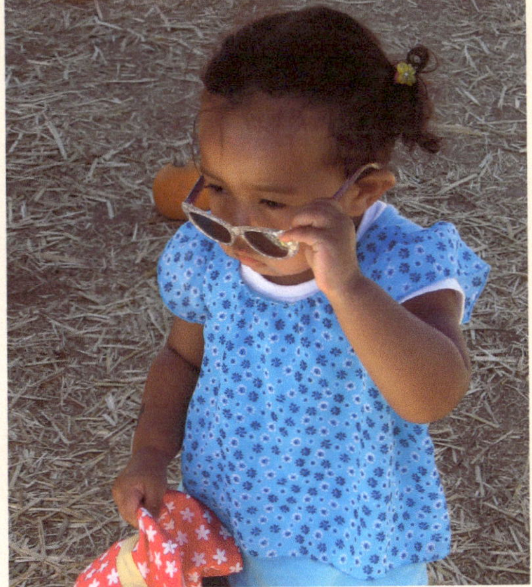

À la Carte Menu

Amuse-bouche
Duck Pâté | Toasted Crostini
COCKTAIL PAIRING: *Brandy Alexander*

First Course: Appetizer
Farro Salad | Kale Greens | Red Beets | Candied Walnuts
Split Pea Soup | Ham
WINE PAIRING: *Dr Heidemanns*
Graacher Kabinett Riesling

Second Course: Entrée
Whipped Russet Potatoes | Garlic | White Cheddar
Baked Wrapped Asparagus | Prosciutto | Gruyere Cheese
Saffron Rice | Raisins | Roasted Pumpkin Seeds
Pan Fried Chicken | Sweet Onion | Roasted Red Peppers
Grilled Filet Mignon | Chasseur Sauce
WINE PAIRING: *Renieri Brunello di Montalcino*
Riserva Sangiovese

Third Course: Dessert
Pumpkin Pie | Spiced Whipped Cream
Mini Carrot Cake | Cream Cheese Walnut Frosting
WINE PAIRING: *Osborne Tawny Port*
ASSORTMENT OF TEAS AND COFFEE

Dining Service Style: *Formal Plated Service*
Guests are seated. Each course will be prepared and
portioned in the kitchen, arranged on china, and served
by servers to the guests. Beverage service will be completed
at tableside by the servers unless there is a designated bar
station. In this instance, the server will obtain a beverage
order, fulfill the order, and serve the beverage to the
guests tableside.

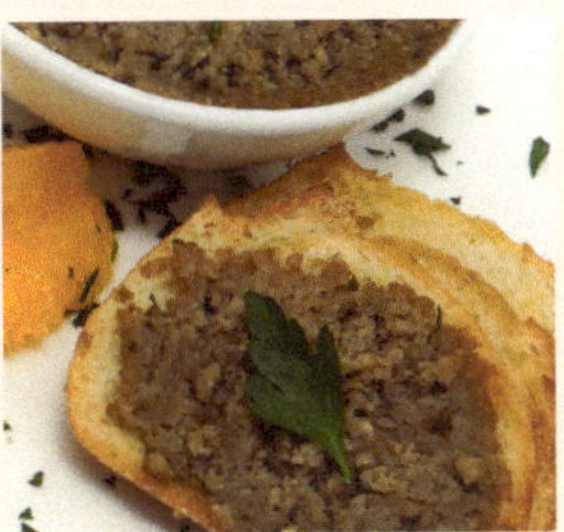

Duck Pâté

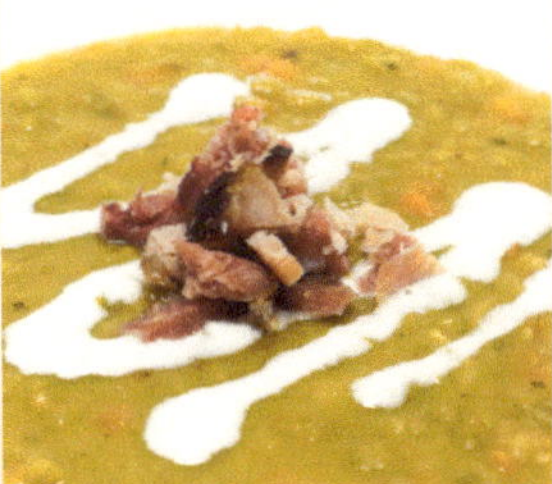

Split Pea Soup

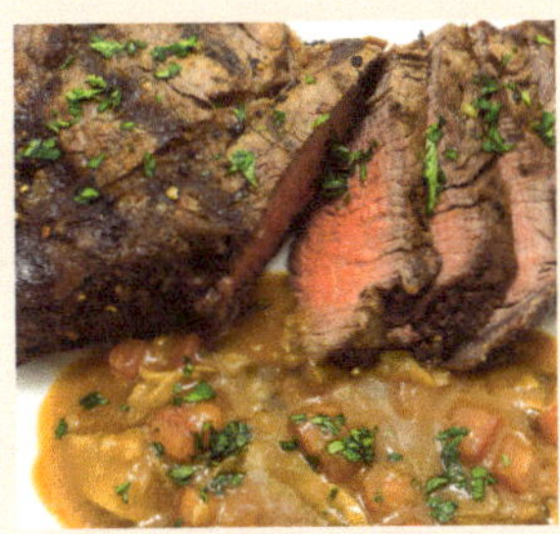

Grilled Filet Mignon

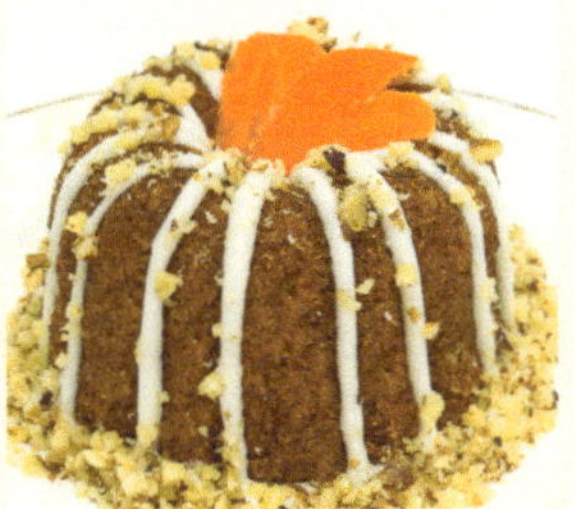

Mini Carrot Cake

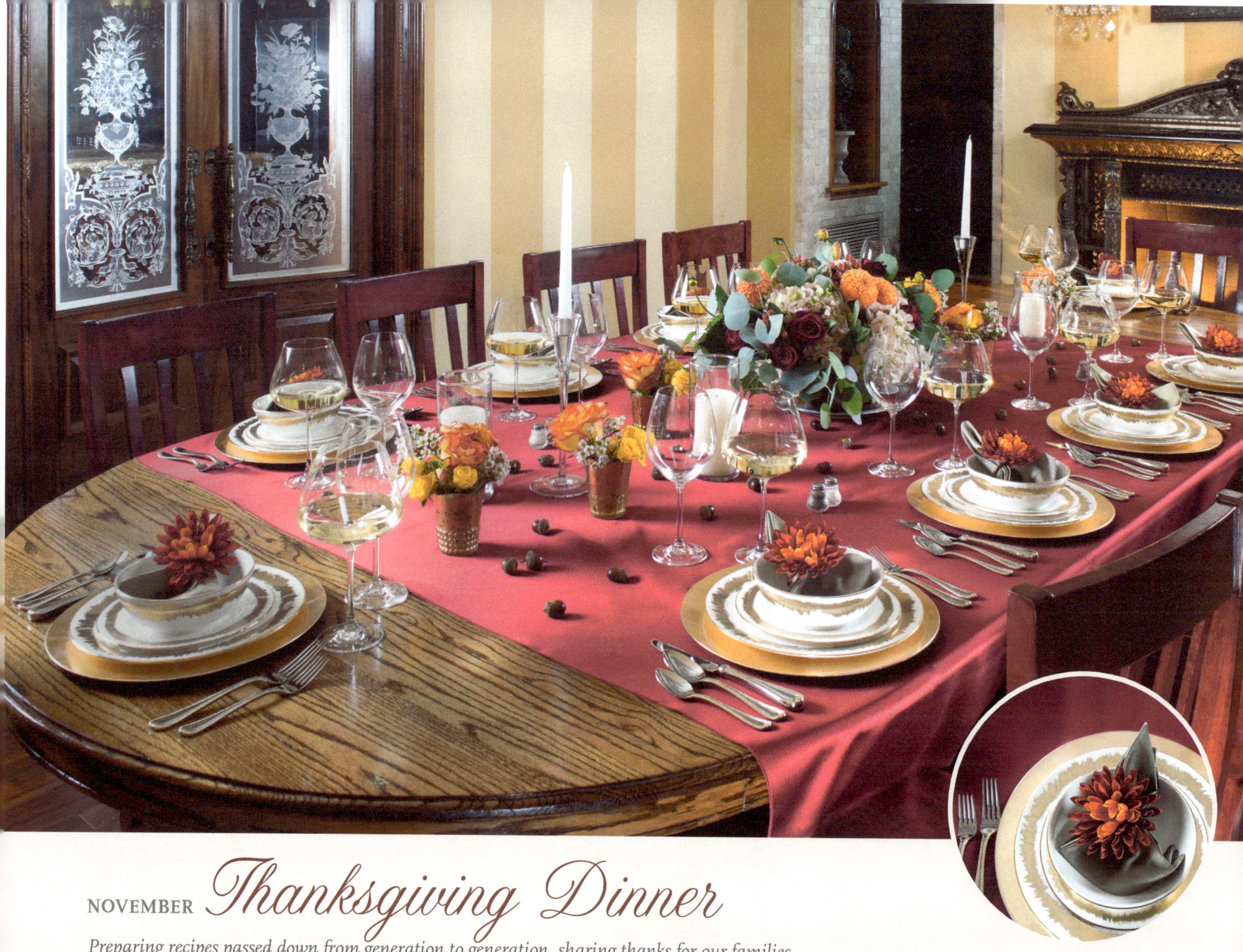

 Thanksgiving Dinner

Preparing recipes passed down from generation to generation, sharing thanks for our families and for each other around this table set for ten.

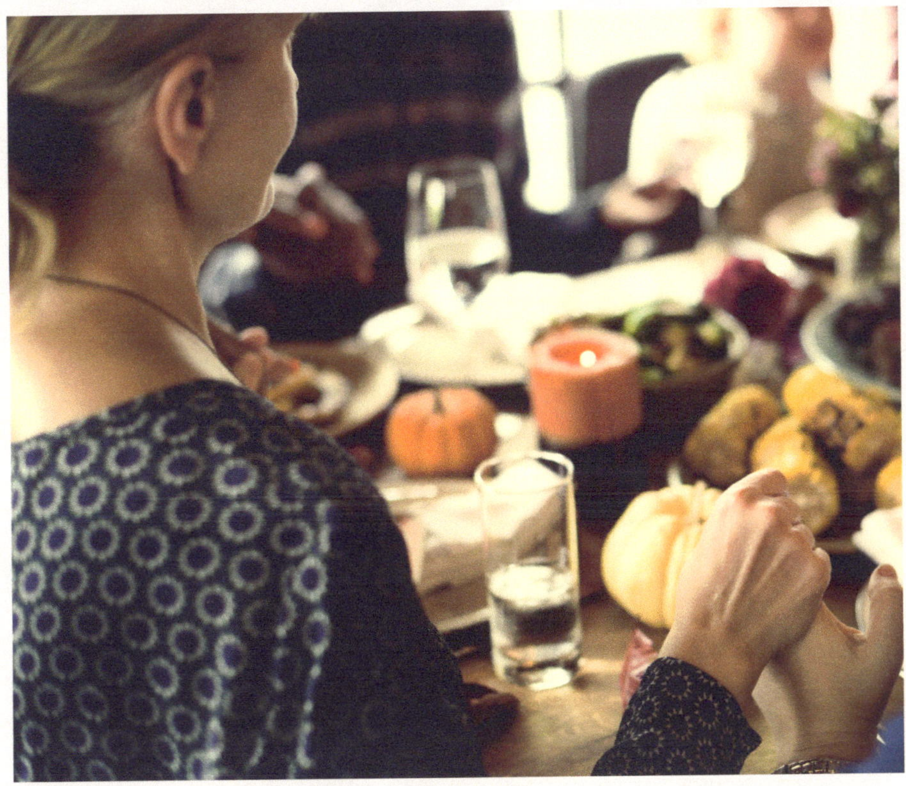

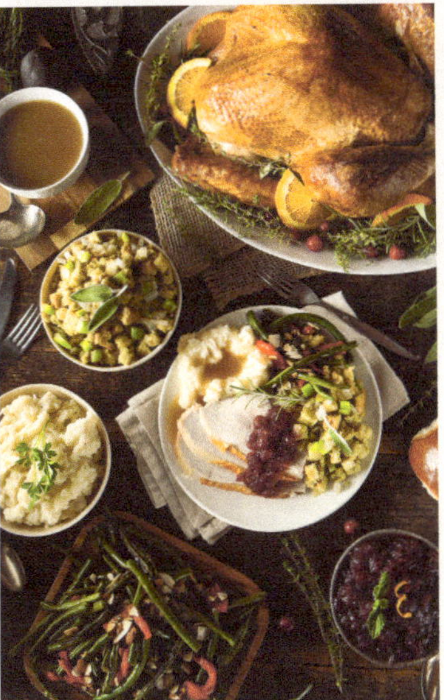

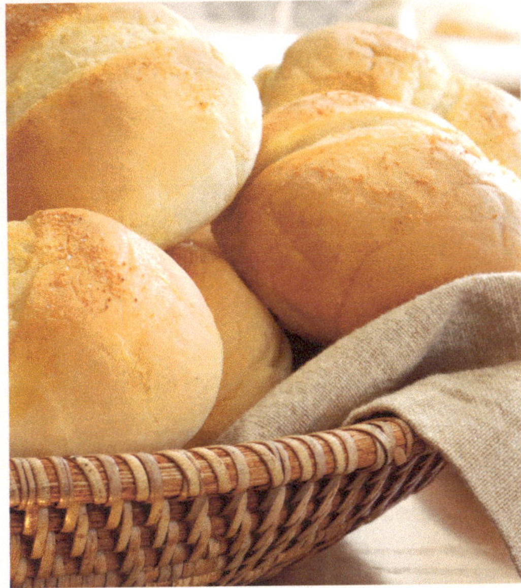

À la Carte Menu

Amuse-bouche
Crispy Collard Greens Chips | Toasted White Sesame Seeds
COCKTAIL PAIRING: *Cosmopolitan*

First Course: Appetizer
Fall Pear Salad | Raspberry Vinaigrette
Butternut Squash Soup | Spicy Sausage & Bell Pepper Confit
WINE PAIRING: *Tesoro della Regina Pinot Grigio*

Second Course: Entrée
Green Beans | Pearl Onions
Cornbread Dressing | Cranberry Orange Relish
Gorgonzola Macaroni and Cheese
Lobster Farrotto
Moroccan Style Baked Tilapia
Roasted Turkey | Root Vegetable Gravy
Grilled Duck | Blood Orange Beurre Blanc Sauce
WINE PAIRING: *Adams Bench Reckoning Merlot*

Third Course: Dessert
Deep Dish Sweet Potato Pie | Pecan Streusel
Velvety Chocolate Grenache Cake | Nougatine Lace
Bavarian Cream
WINE PAIRING: *Quinta das Carvalhas Reserva Tawny Port*
ASSORTMENT OF TEAS AND COFFEE

Dining Service Style: *Family Style Service*
with Server Assistance
Guests are seated. Large serving platters and bowls are
filled with foods in the kitchen and set on the dining
tables by servers. Guests help themselves as they pass the
foods to each other. Beverages are served to the guests
administered at tableside.

Course highlights:

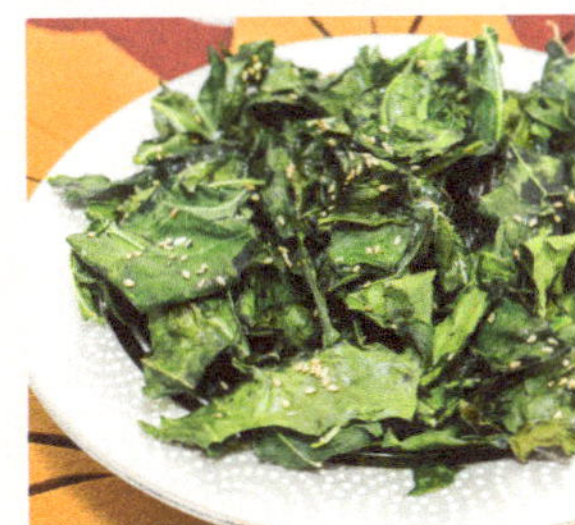

Crispy Collard Greens Chips

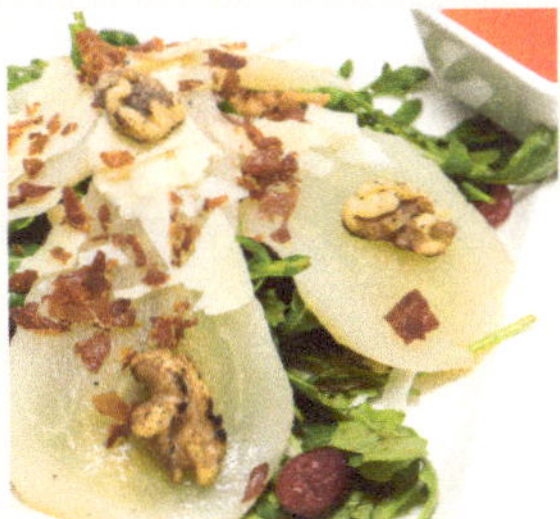

Fall Pear Salad

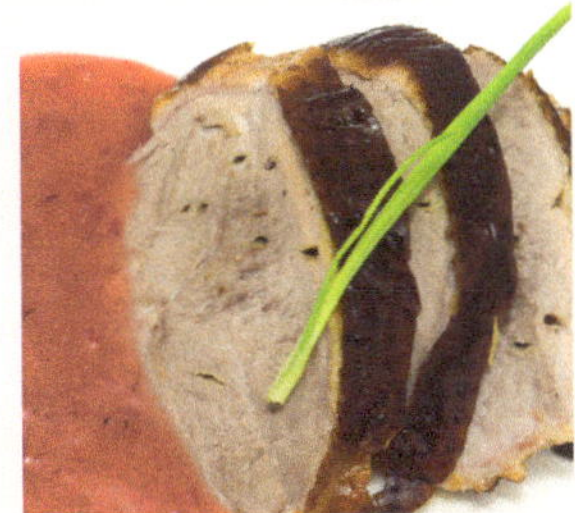

Grilled Duck

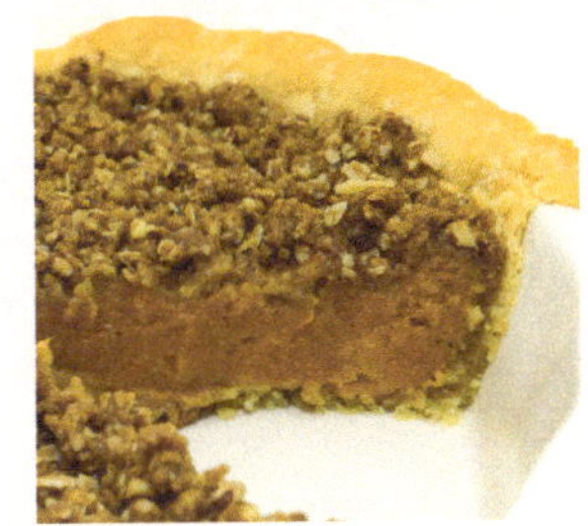

Deep Dish Sweet Potato Pie

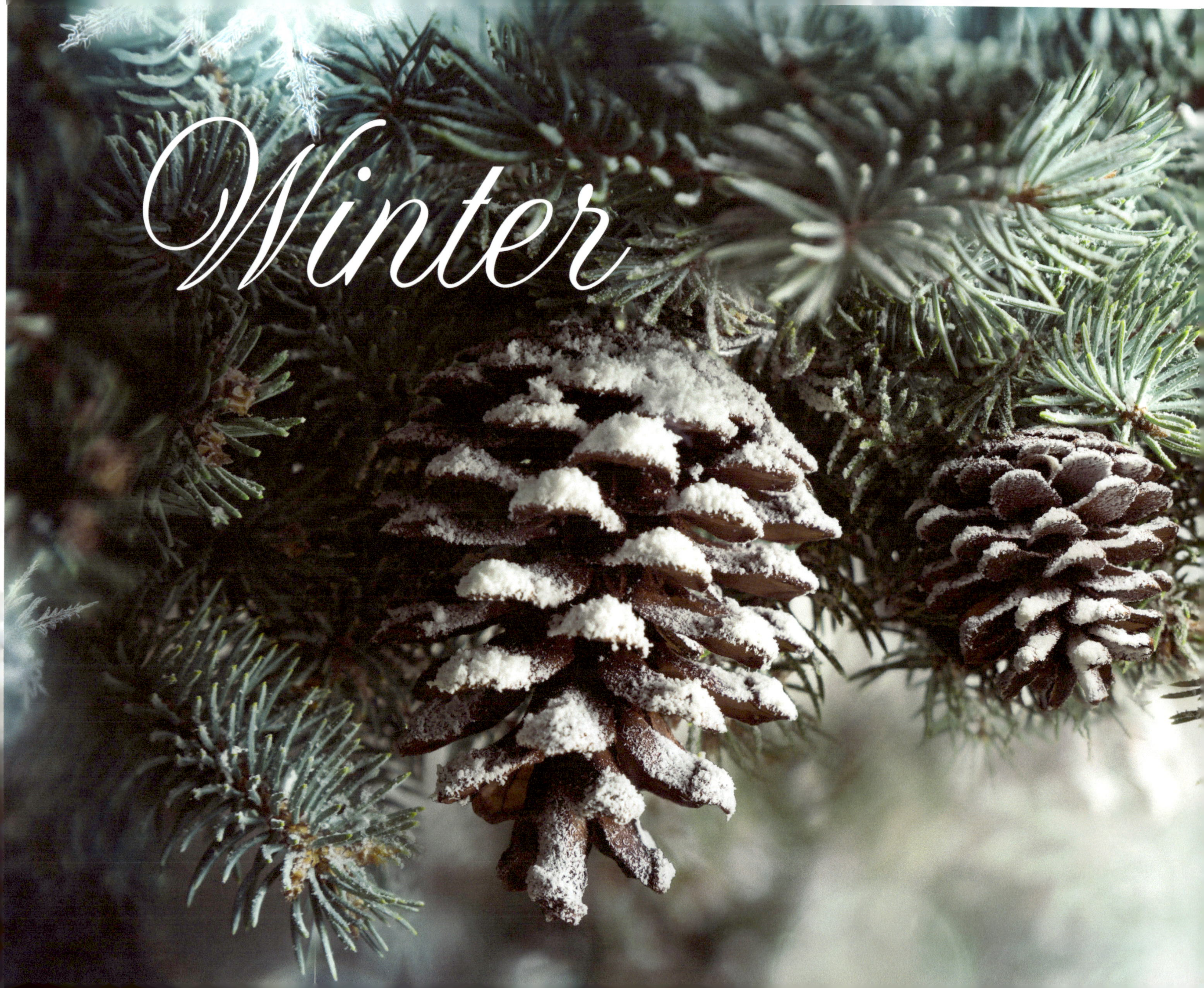
Winter

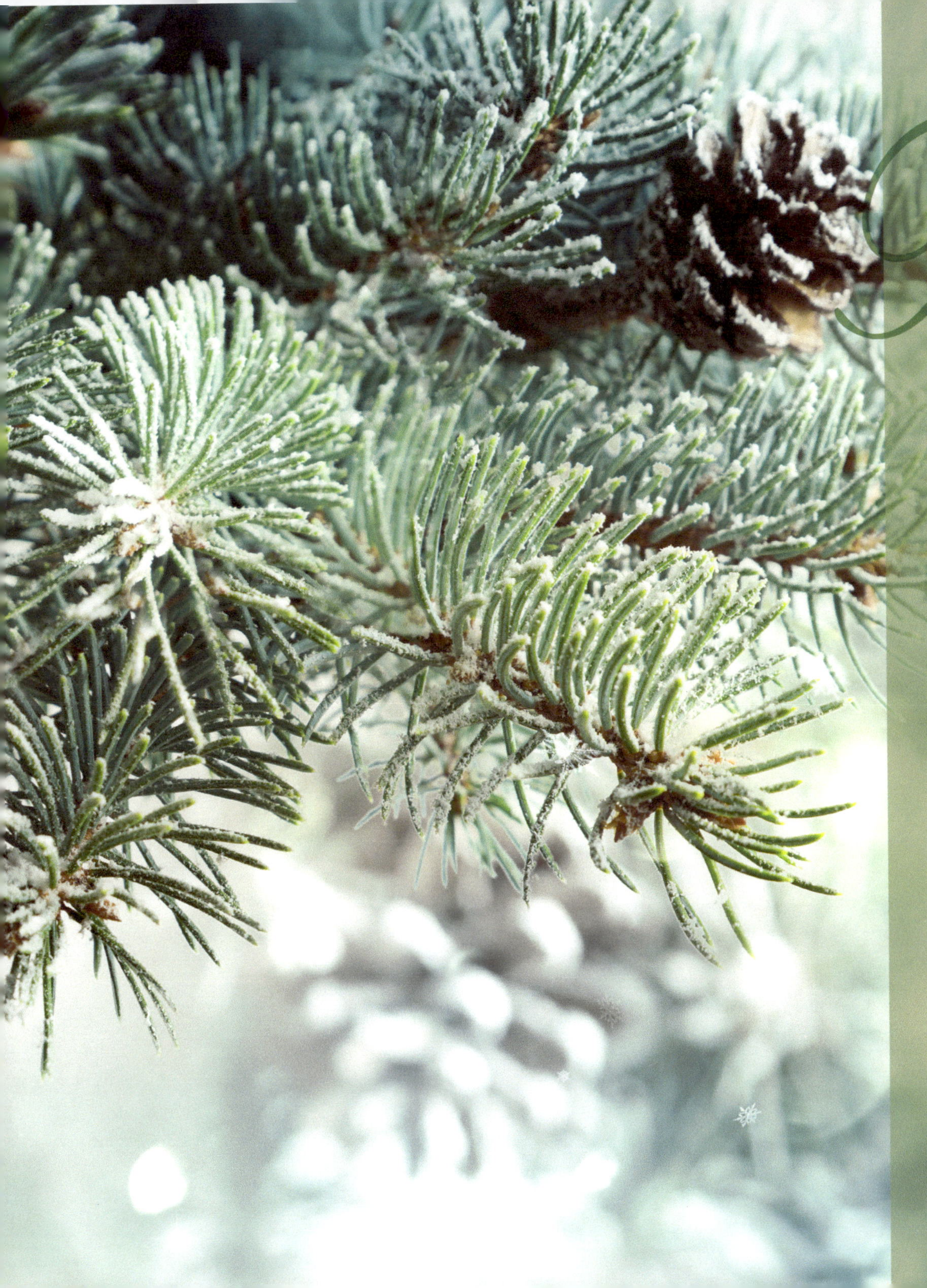

The family gathers at the table for a home-cooked holiday dinner with the magnificence of the meal in full display. The smells of eggnog and spiced apple cider greet guests at the door, promising to warm their bones from the crisp, frosty air. The aroma of pine from freshly-cut trees and wreaths alert your senses yet leave you feeling peaceful and tranquil. Icicles line the gutters and hang from trees, decorating the now-barren landscape. Children play in the snow, making snowmen and snow angels, while adults go caroling to bring in the festive season.

Winter is a time when we reflect on the year past and anticipate the new year approaching.

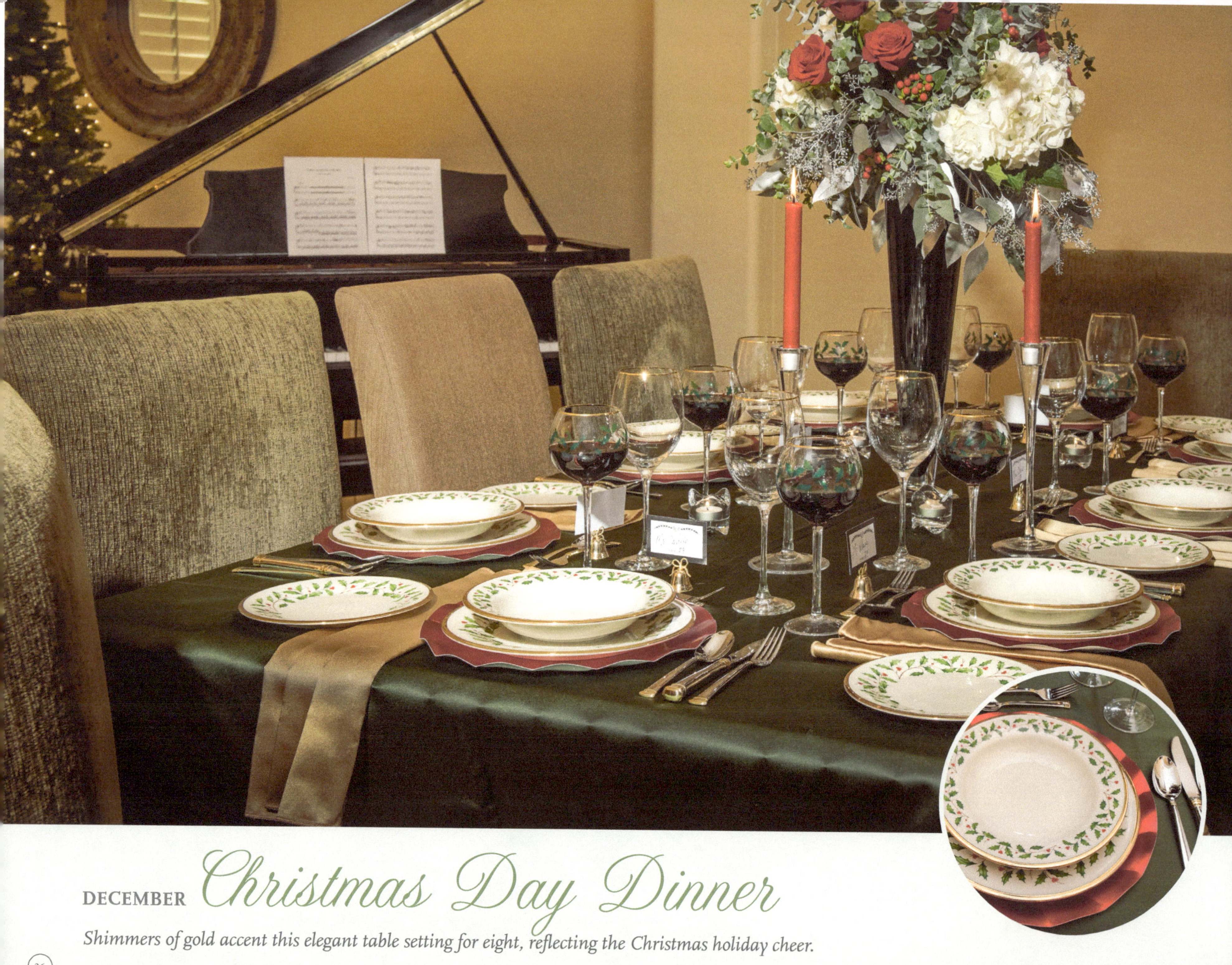

 Christmas Day Dinner

Shimmers of gold accent this elegant table setting for eight, reflecting the Christmas holiday cheer.

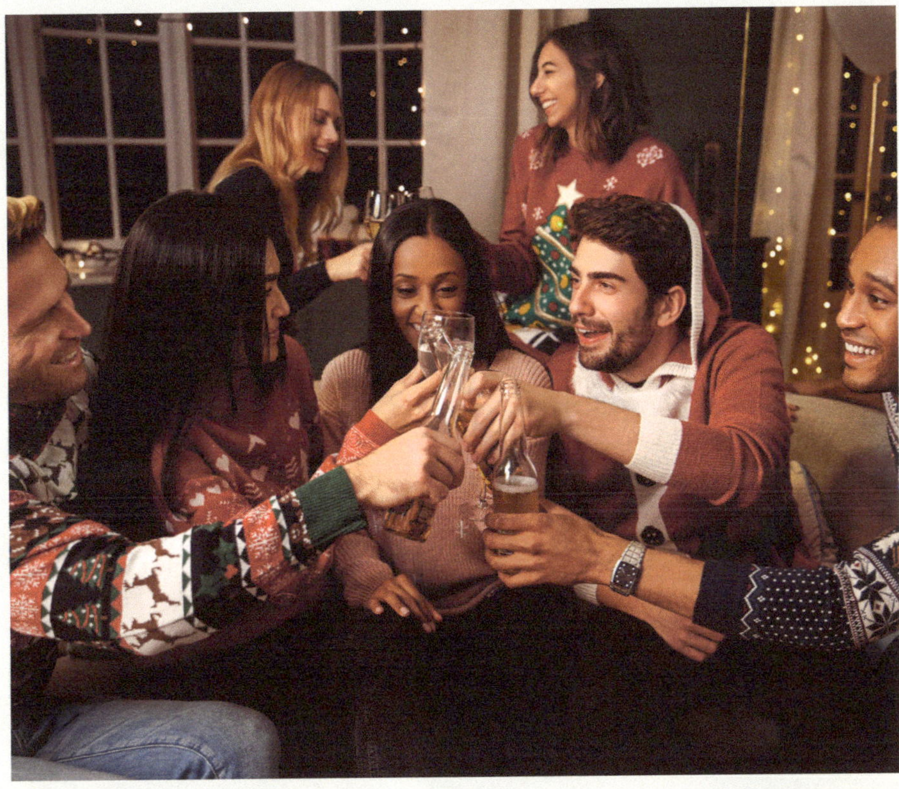

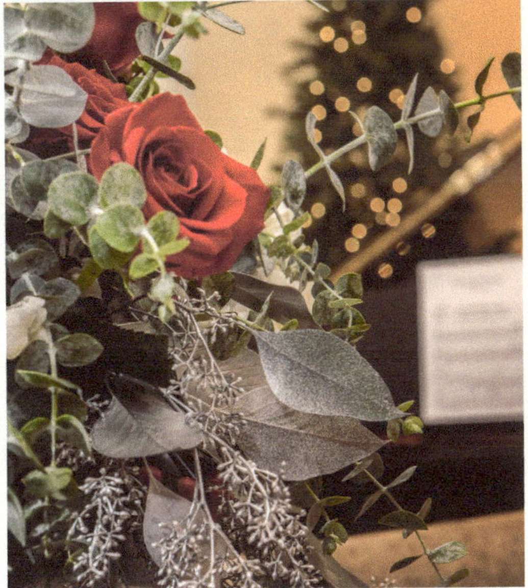

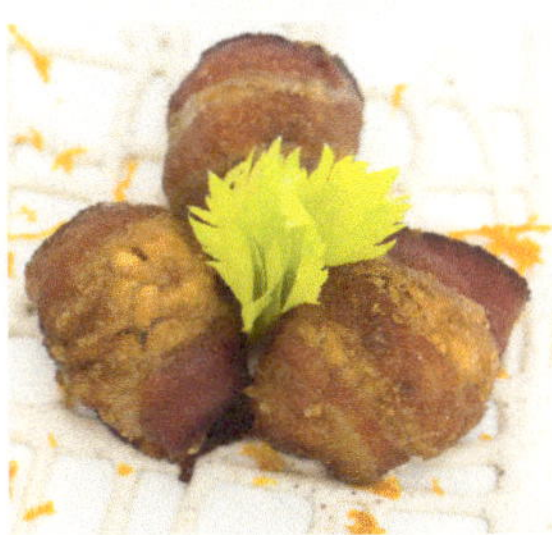

Roasted Bacon-Wrapped Italian Chestnuts

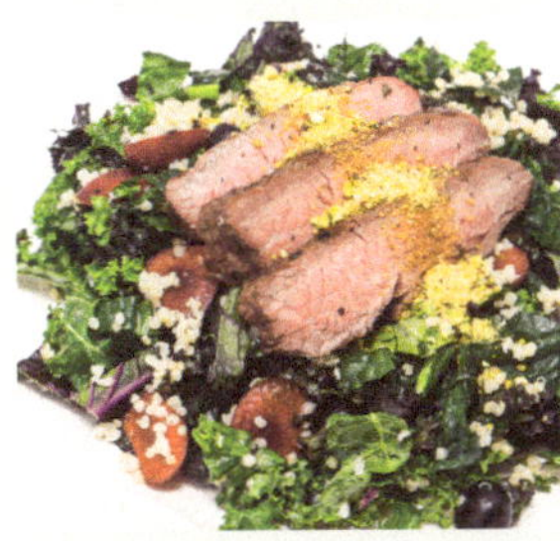

Quinoa, Kale, Flank Steak Salad

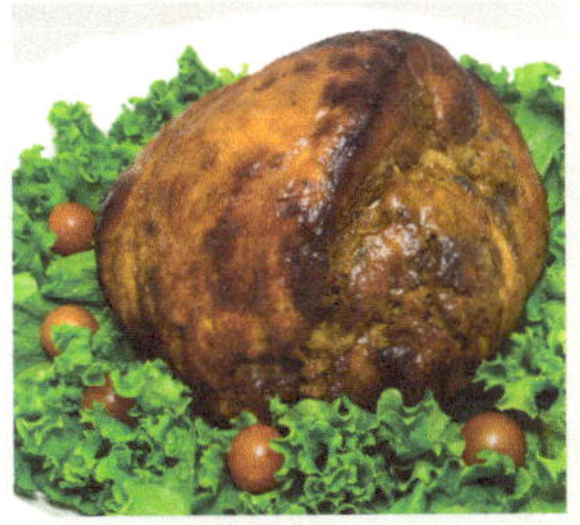

Citrus Glazed Stuffed Corned Ham

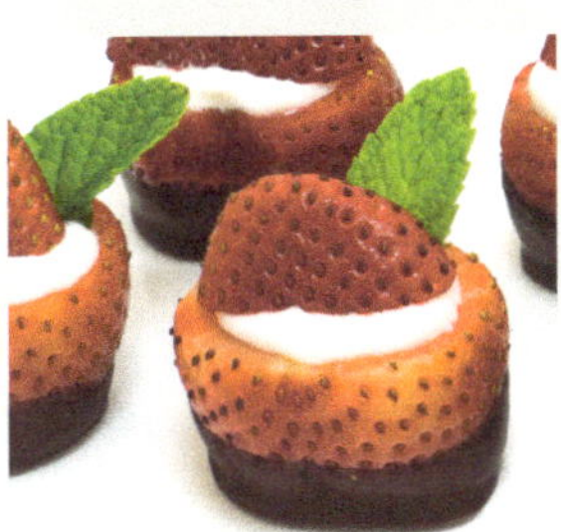

Chocolate Dipped Strawberries

À la Carte Menu

Amuse-bouche
Roasted Bacon-Wrapped Italian Chestnuts
Mascarpone Cheese & Orange Zest
> COCKTAIL PAIRING: *Cognac Spiced Apple Cider*
> *with Cinnamon Stick*

First Course: Appetizer
Quinoa, Kale, Flank Steak Salad | Champagne Vinaigrette
Whole Grain Farro and Tri Tip Beef Stew
> WINE PAIRING: *Allegrini Amarone della*
> *Valpolicella Classico Red Wine*

Second Course: Entrée
Coconut Rice Patties
Baked Eggplant | Marinara Sauce
Sautéed Broccolini | Parmesan Shavings
Roasted Cornish Hens | Mushroom Duxelles Stuffing
Red Pepper Coulis
Caribbean Grilled Red Snapper
Citrus Glazed Stuffed Corned Ham
> WINE PAIRING: *Jemrose Viognier Egret White Wine*

Third Course: Dessert
Chocolate Dipped Strawberries
Lemon Whipped Cream Filling | Mint
Red Velvet Cake | Vanilla Pastry Cream | Cream Cheese Frosting
> WINE PAIRING: *Mailly 'Delice' Demi-Sec*
> *Grand Cru Champagne*
> ASSORTMENT OF TEAS AND COFFEE

Dining Service Style: *Formal Plated Service*
Each course will be prepared and portioned in the kitchen, arranged on china, and served by servers to the guests. Beverage service will be completed at tableside by the servers unless there is a designated bar station. In this instance, the server will obtain a beverage order, fulfill the order, and serve the beverage to the guests tableside.

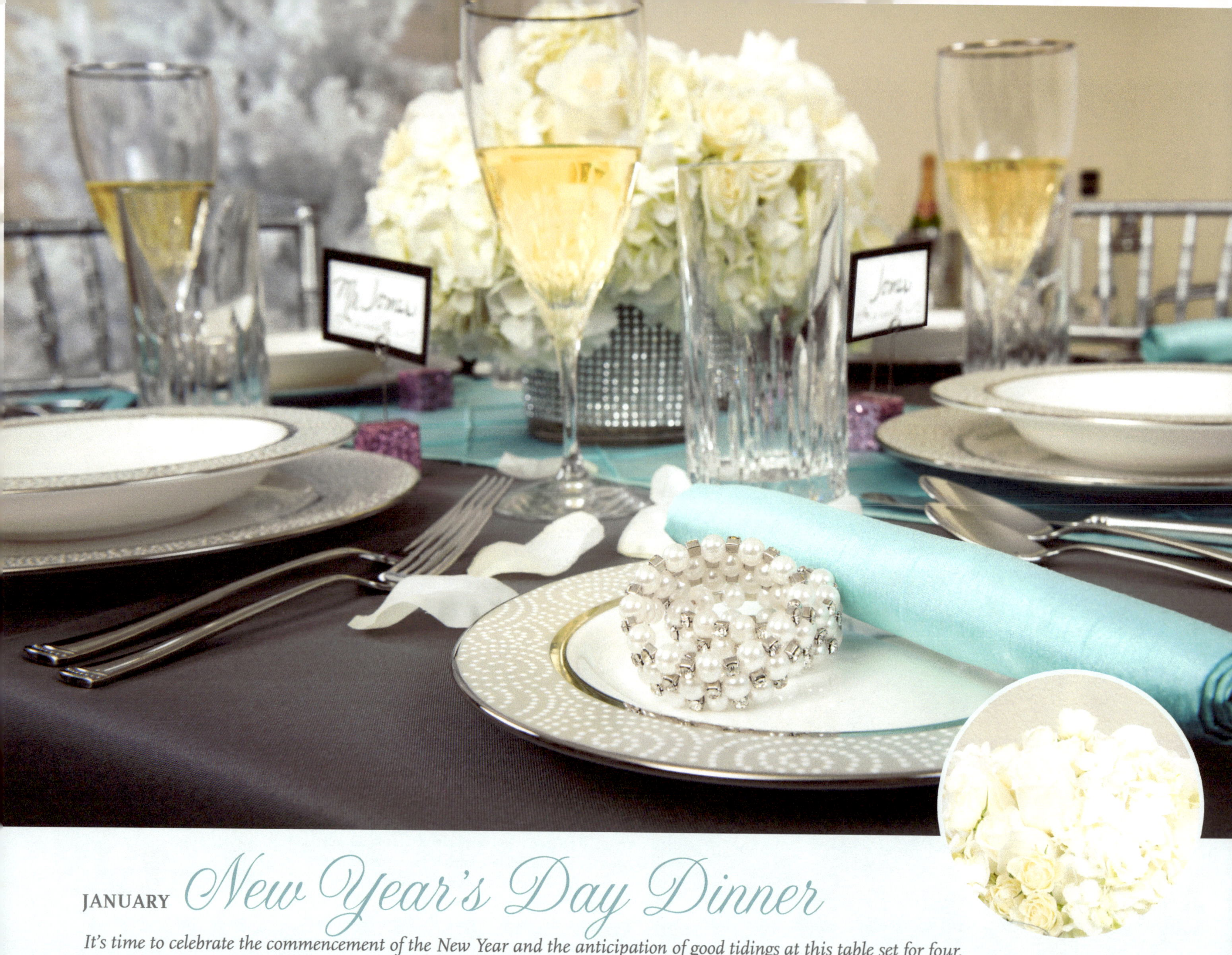

JANUARY *New Year's Day Dinner*

It's time to celebrate the commencement of the New Year and the anticipation of good tidings at this table set for four.

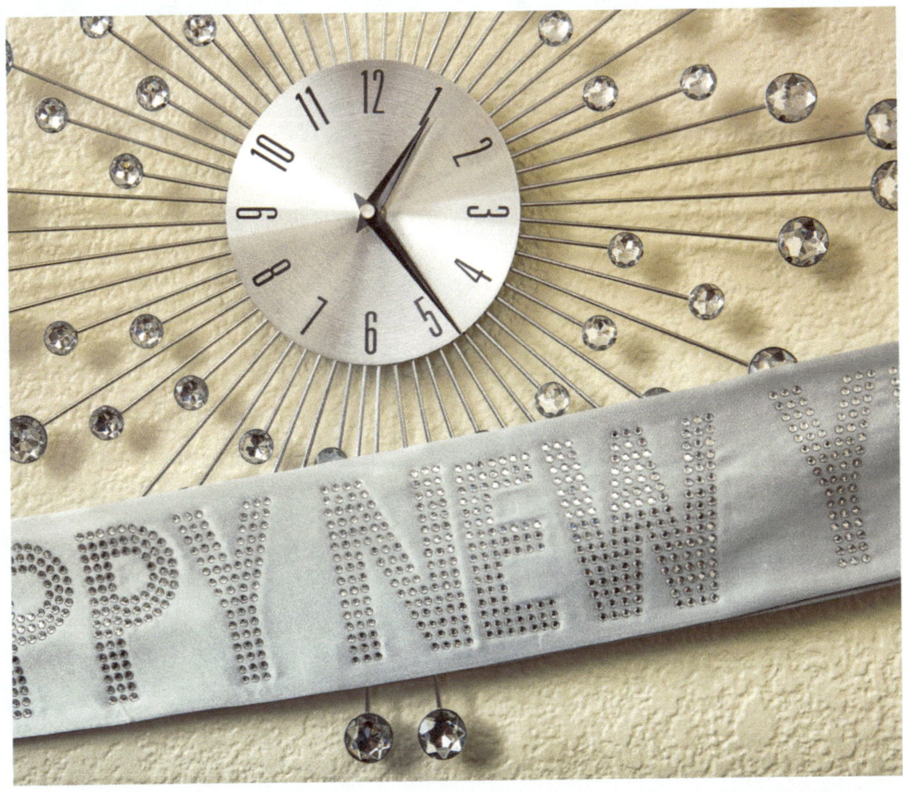

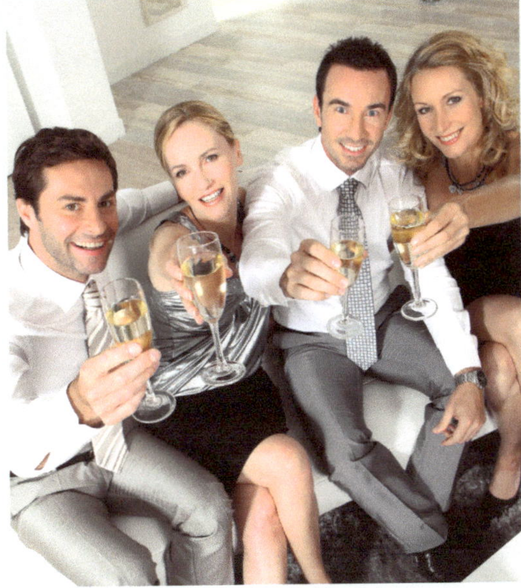

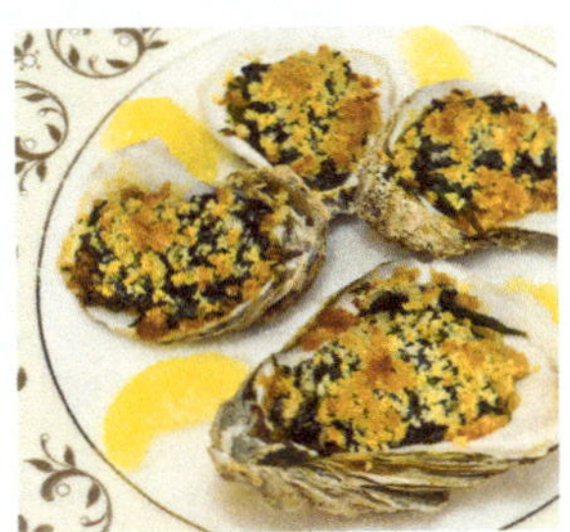

Oysters Rockefeller

À la Carte Menu

Amuse-bouche
Oysters Rockefeller | Kosher Salt Bed
   COCKTAIL PAIRING: *Chilled Sake*

First Course: Appetizer
Black-Eyed Pea Salad | Balsamic Glaze &
Red Wine Vinaigrette
Pea Soup | Bacon and Shrimp Confit
   WINE PAIRING: *Montaudon Classe 'M' Champagne*

Second Course: Entrée
Rice Pilaf | Vegetables
Duchess Potatoes
Braised Endive and Radicchio | White Wine
Mushroom Diane | Assorted Greens
Roasted Capone | Dried Fruit & Nut Stuffing
First Cut Boneless Ribeye Roast | Marchand de Vin Sauce
   WINE PAIRING: *Chateau Kirwan Margaux Bordeaux Blend*

Third Course: Dessert
Poached Pears | Vanilla Bean Ice Cream
Roquefort Cheese | Candied Pecans
   WINE PAIRING: *Marchese dell'Elsa Moscato d'Asti*
   ASSORTMENT OF TEAS AND COFFEE

Dining Service Style: *Formal Plated Service*
Each course will be prepared and portioned in the kitchen, arranged on china, and served by servers to the guests. Beverage service will be completed at tableside by the servers unless there is a designated bar station. In this instance, the server will obtain a beverage order, fulfill the order, and serve the beverage to the guests tableside.

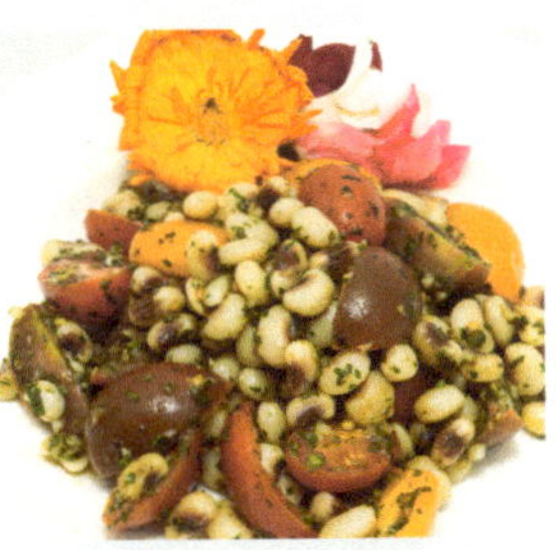

Black-Eyed Pea Salad

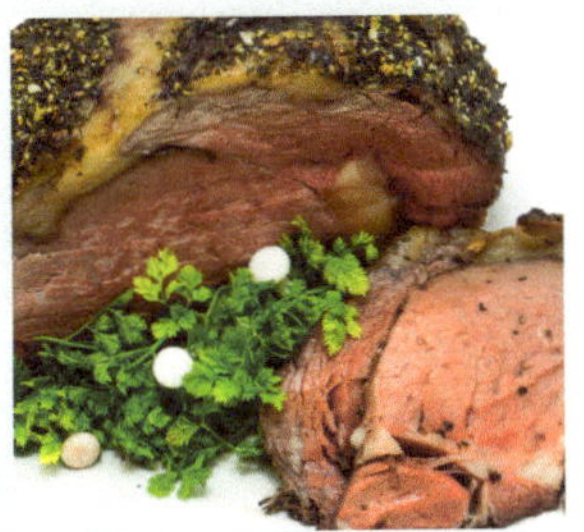

First Cut Boneless Ribeye Roast

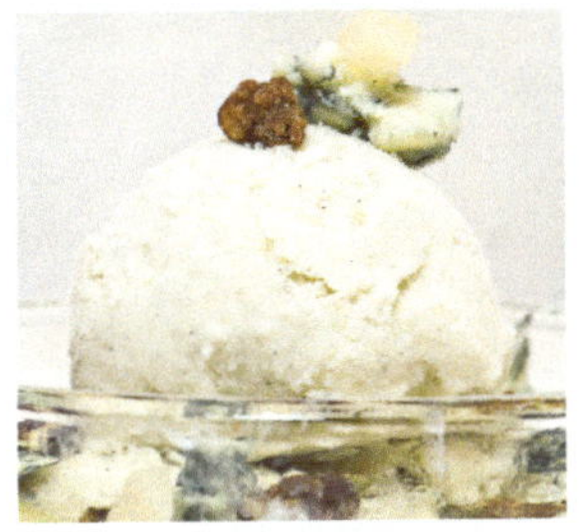

Poached Pear Vanilla Bean Ice Cream

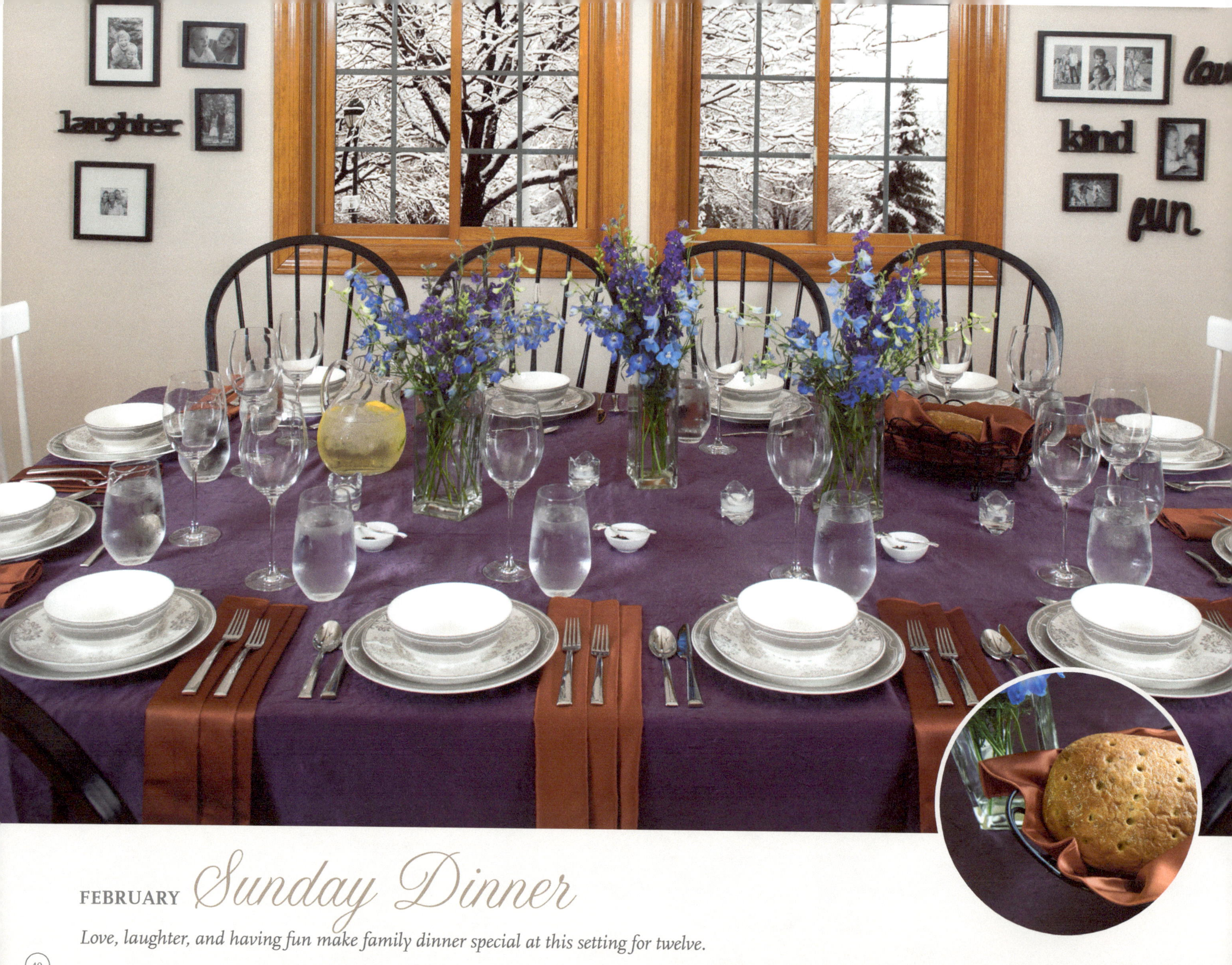

FEBRUARY Sunday Dinner

Love, laughter, and having fun make family dinner special at this setting for twelve.

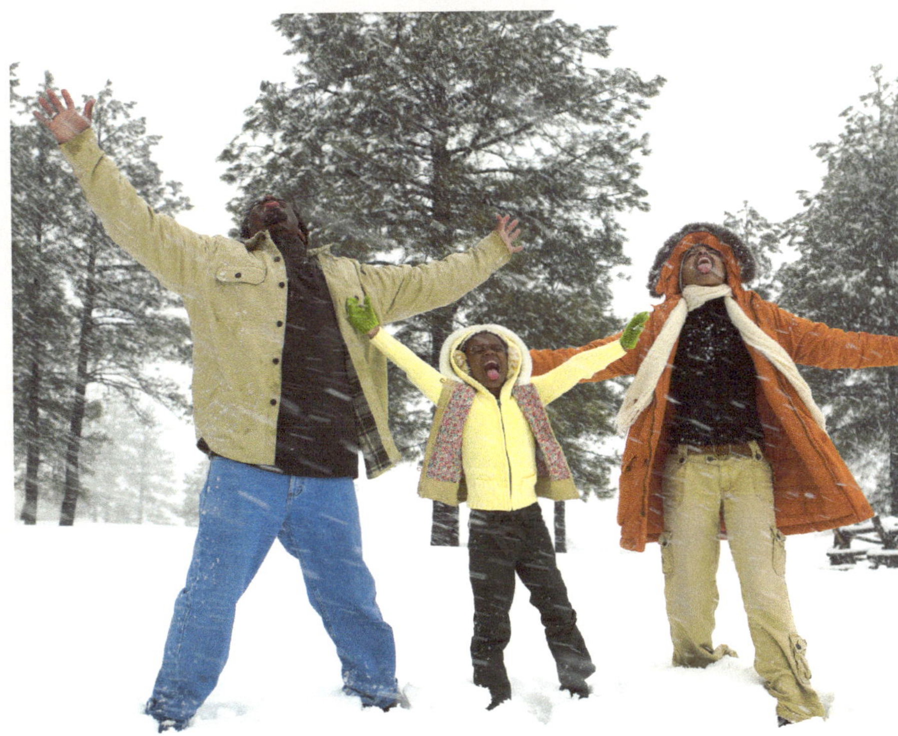

À la Carte Menu

Amuse-bouche
Corned Beef Hash Cabbage Roll | Marinara Sauce
COCKTAIL PAIRING: *Mini Bloody Mary's*

First Course: Appetizer
Sausage, Chicken, and Seafood Gumbo | Saffron Rice
WINE PAIRING: *Macchia Zinfandel Adventurous*

Second Course: Entrée
Yam Casserole | Marshmallows
Fried Corn | Bacon | Bell Peppers
Warmed Kale | Pork Shavings
Sautéed Okra | Sweet Onion | Garlic
Chicken & Dumplings
Braised Beef Short Ribs | Varietal Squash Ribbons
Braised Oxtails | Seasonal Vegetables
WINE PAIRING: *Amadieu Romane Machotte*
Gigondas Red Wine

Third Course: Dessert
Peach Cobbler | Vanilla Ice Cream
Yellow Pound Cake | Fresh Berries
WINE PAIRING: *Chateau de la Roulerie*
Coteaux du Layon Chenin Blanc
ASSORTMENT OF TEAS AND COFFEE

Dining Service Style: *Family Style Service with Server Assistance*
Guests are seated. Large serving platters and bowls are filled with foods in the kitchen and set on the dining tables by servers. Guests help themselves as they pass the foods to each other. Beverages are served to the guests.

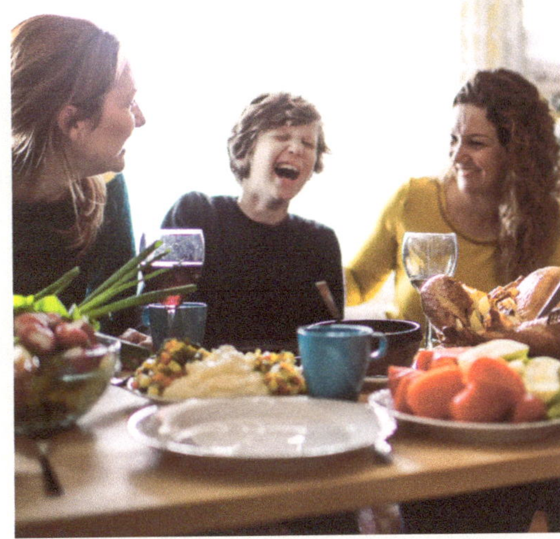

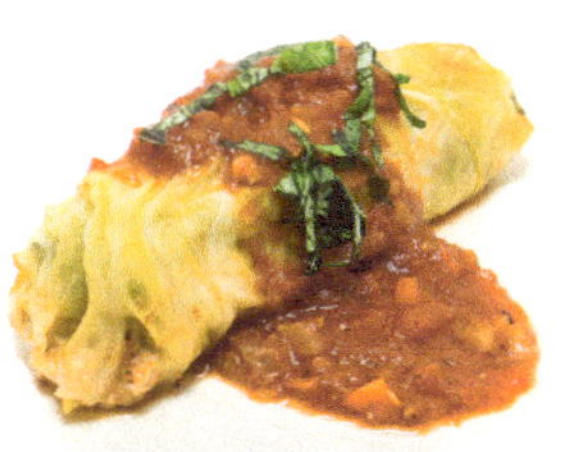

Corned Beef Hash Cabbage Roll

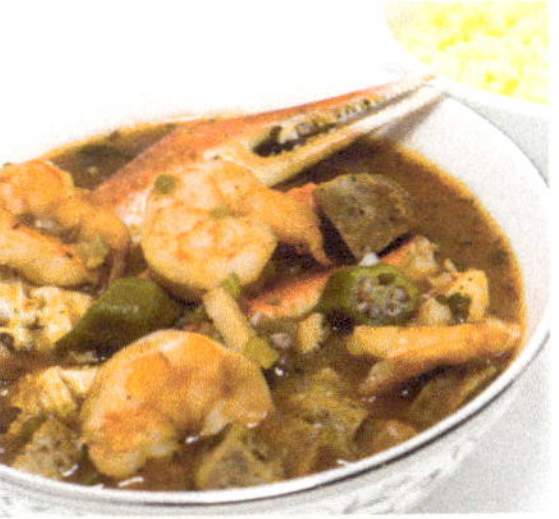

Sausage, Chicken, and Seafood Gumbo

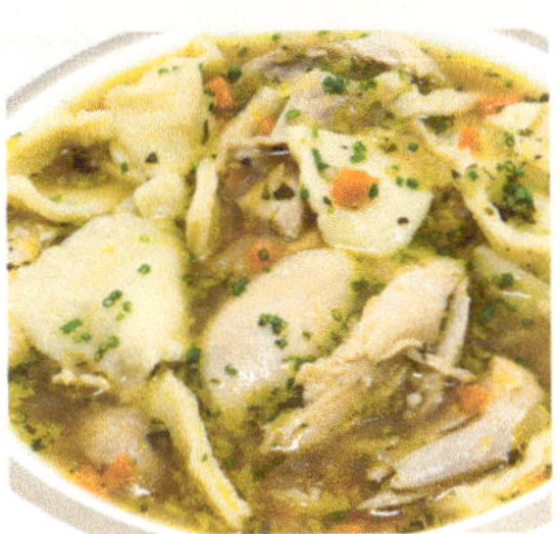

Chicken & Dumplings

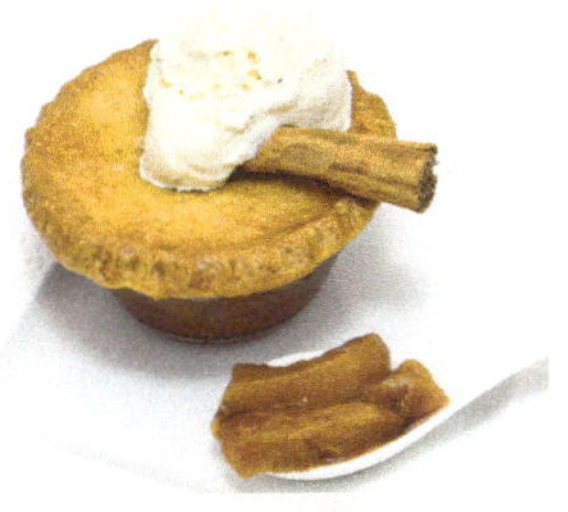

Peach Cobbler

Your Cheerleaders: Keep Them Close

I want to say a special thank you to the many friends and family members who have supported this endeavor from the beginning. I think of them as my cheerleaders. Without their encouragement and steadfastness, my career change might not have happened and I might not have achieved the mission of this book.

They have listened to every story. They have wiped away my tears. They have helped to keep my family routine intact as I embarked on the various paths this journey has taken me. So, thank you, my dear cheerleaders, for your steady support and love.

I want to emphasize the importance of keeping like-minded, positive people around you as your cheerleaders when you are striving for a goal. Taking on a new challenge can be scary and daunting. There are days you may talk yourself right out of it and want to go back to the status quo. However, giving up means that you will not reach your full potential.

This is why your cheerleaders are so important. They push you forward. They hold you accountable. They help you stand when you just want to sit. They lift your spirits when you are down. They remind you to take one day at a time and to keep your eye on the goal.

Keep your cheerleaders close by—and on speed dial.

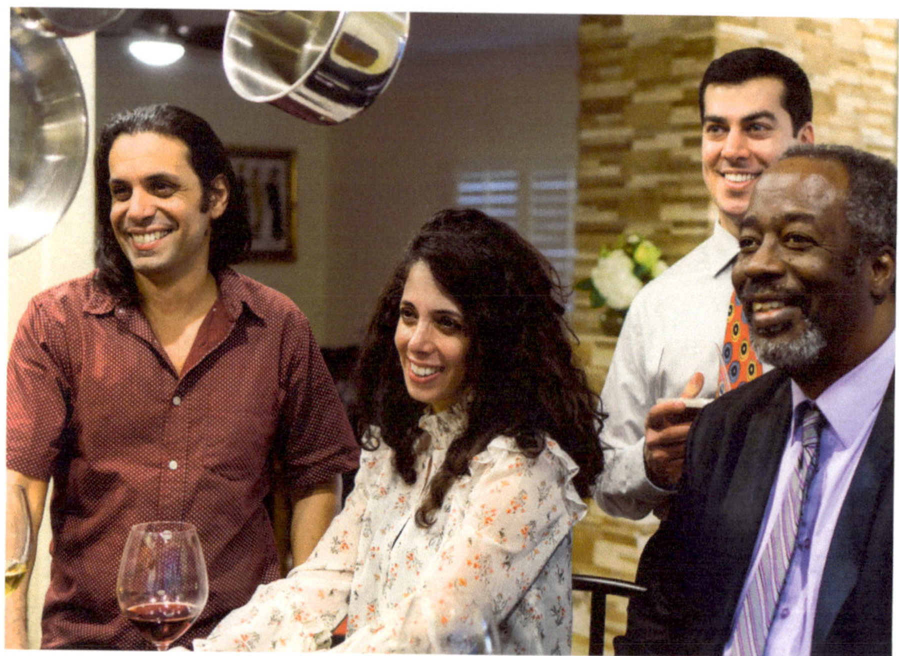

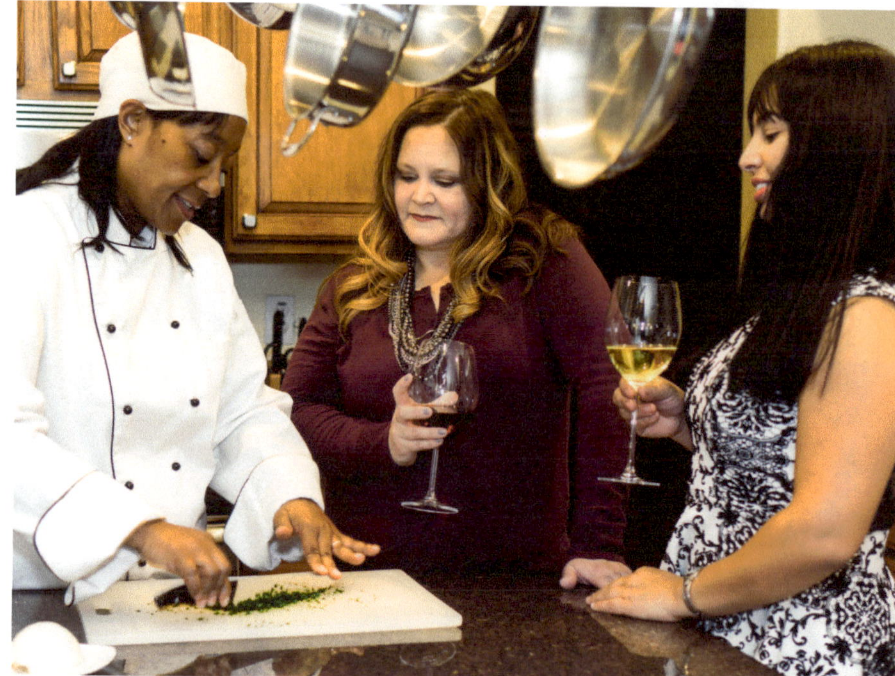

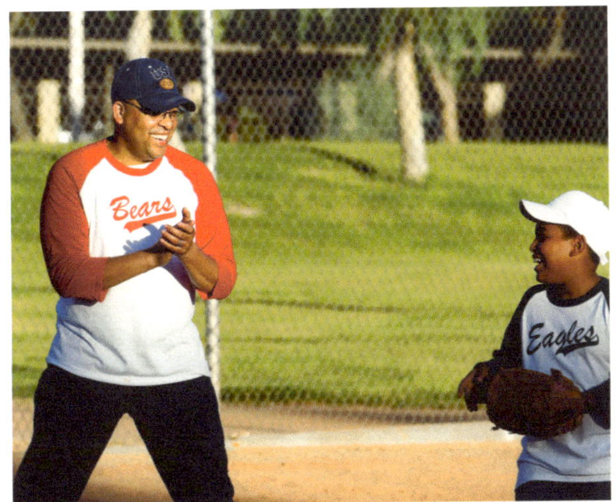

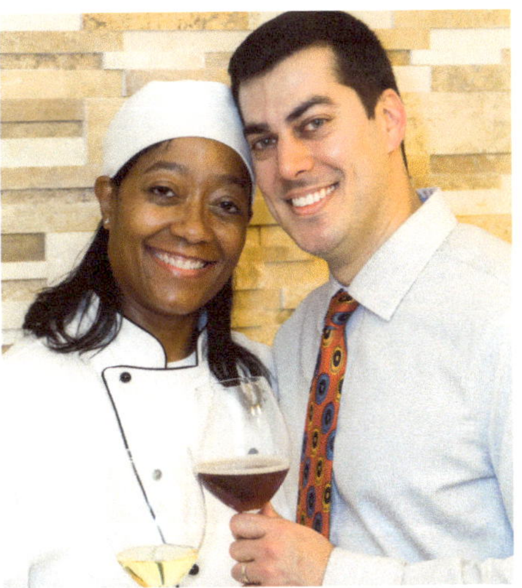

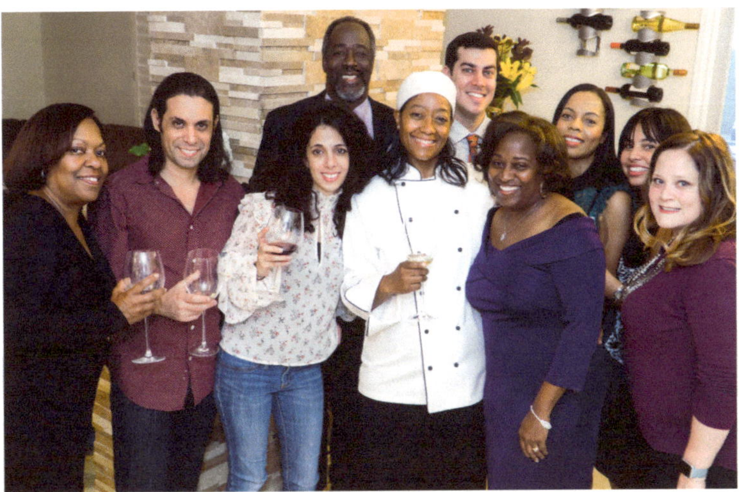

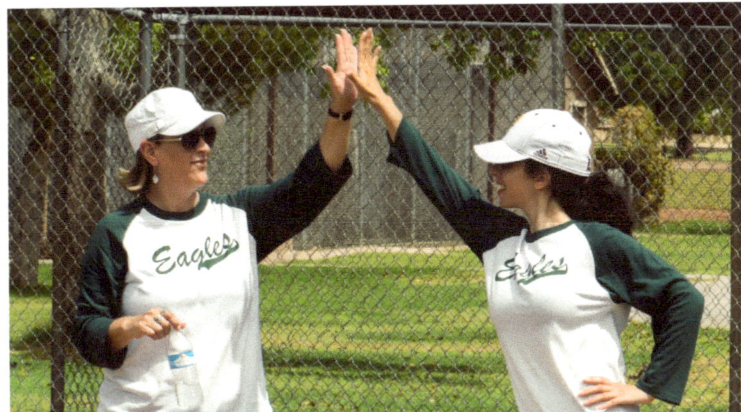

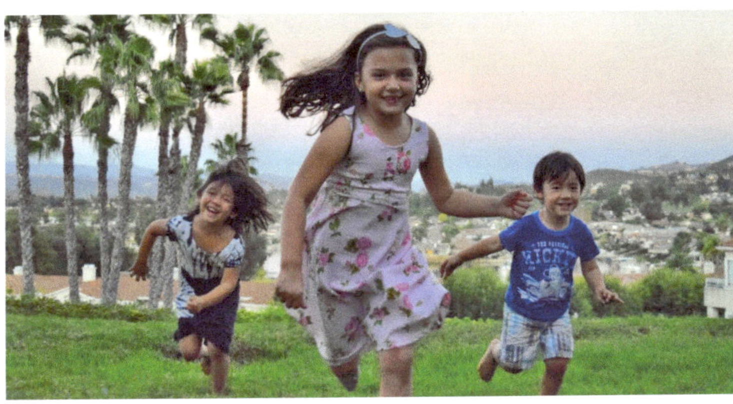

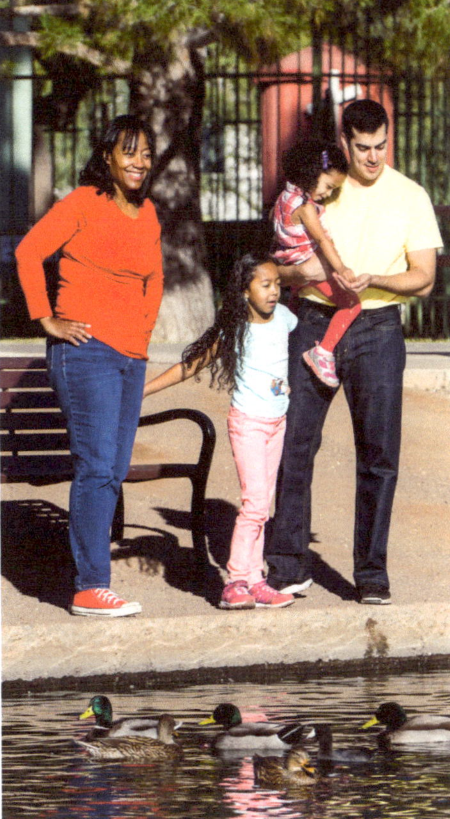

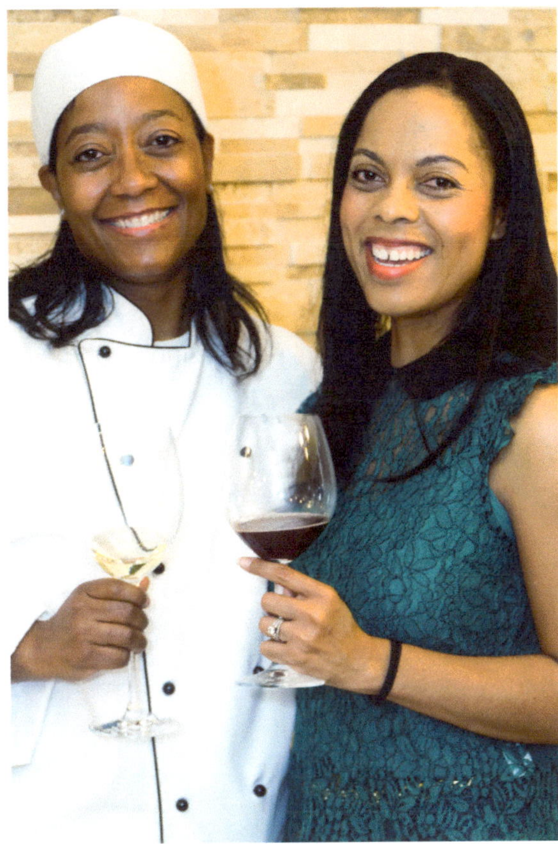

Appendix: Lenox China Highlighted in the Book

March: *Easter Brunch*

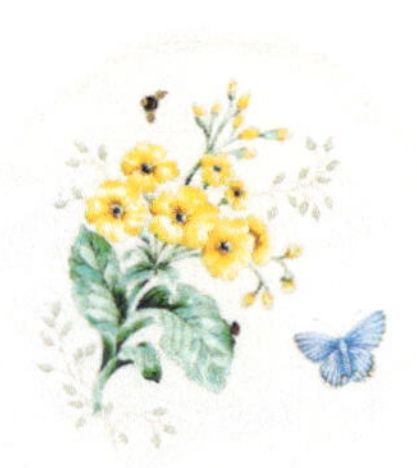

Butterfly Meadow Accent Plate
6140909, 6083661, 6083786, 6083422, 6140933, 6083547

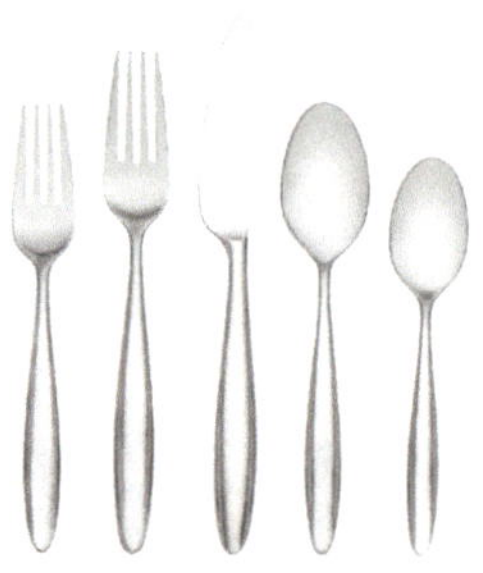

Curve 5 Piece Place Setting
823594

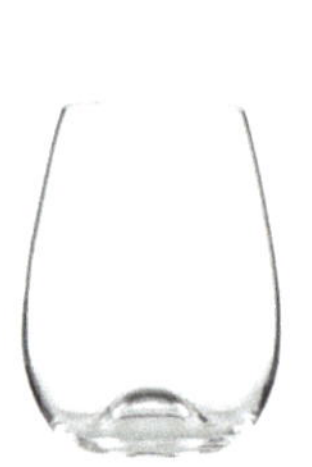

Tuscany Classics All
Purpose Stemless s/6
841689

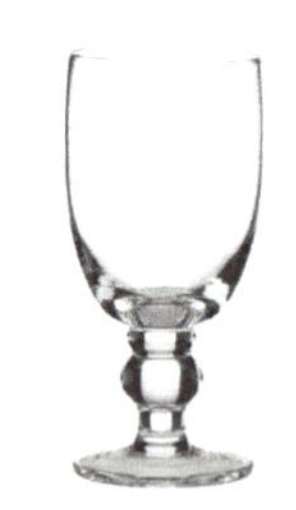

Tuscany Classics Casual
All Purpose s/4
857765

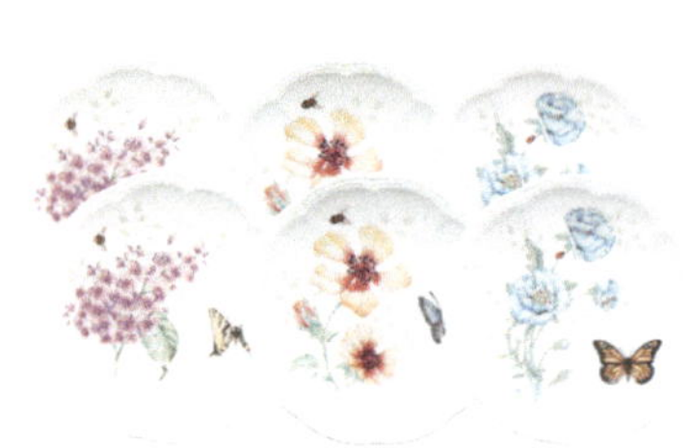

Butterfly Meadow Party Plates s/6
817046

April: *Springtime Brunch*

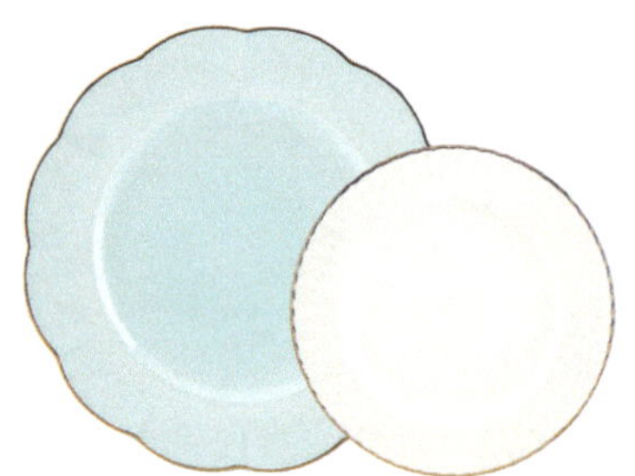

Marchesa Shades of Teal Dinner Plate
Marchesa Shades of White Party Plate
858492, 858574

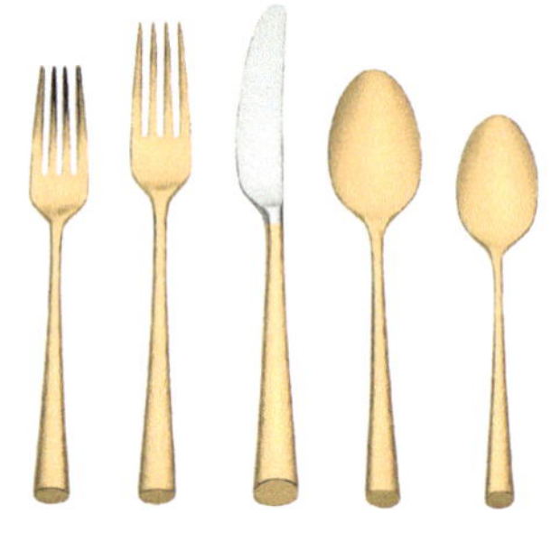

Marchesa Imperial Caviar Gold 5 Piece Place Setting
831900

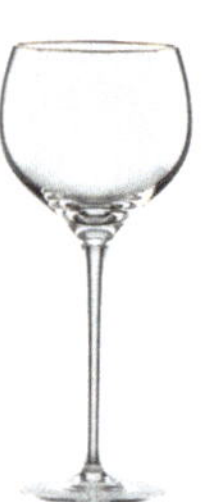

Eternal Gold
Signature Wine
818327

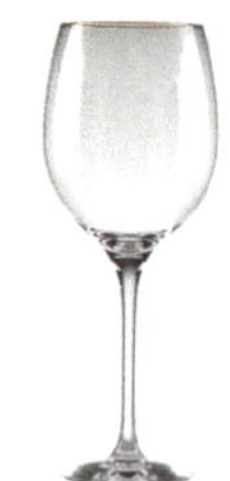

Eternal Gold Signature
All Purpose Beverage
818325

May: *Mother's Day Brunch*

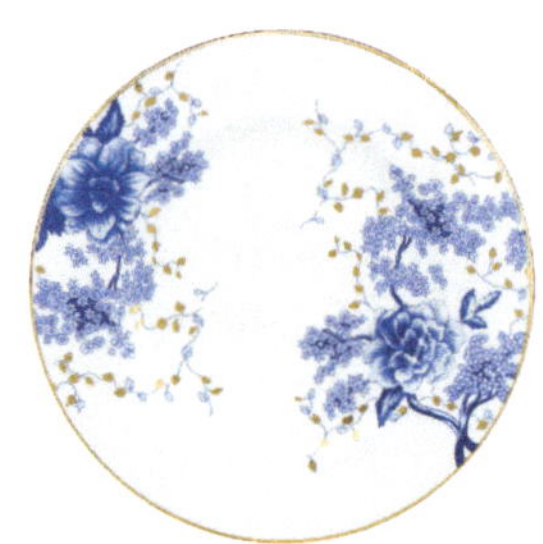

Garden Grove Salad Plate
834259

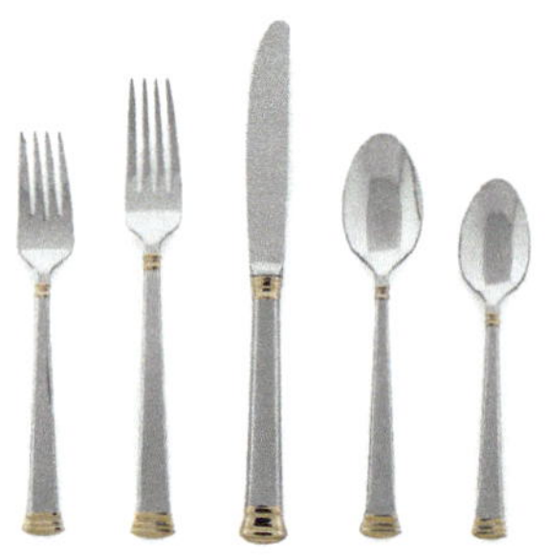

Eternal Gold 5 Piece Place Setting
9828092

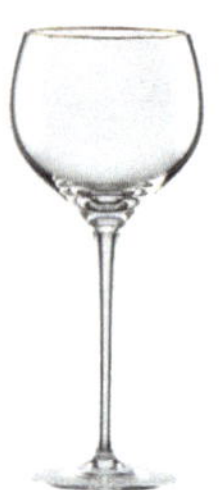

Eternal Gold
Signature Wine
818327

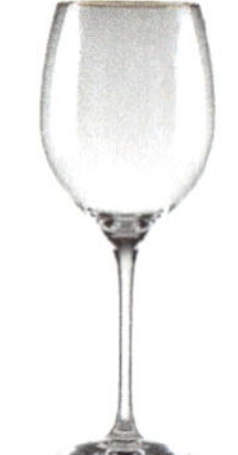

Eternal Gold Signature All
Purpose Beverage
818325

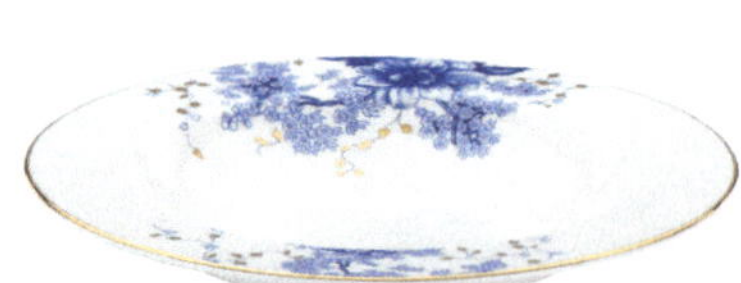

Garden Grove Pasta / Rim Soup Bowl
834257

June: *Romantic Dinner at the Beach*

Opal Innocence Silver Dinner Plate
834209

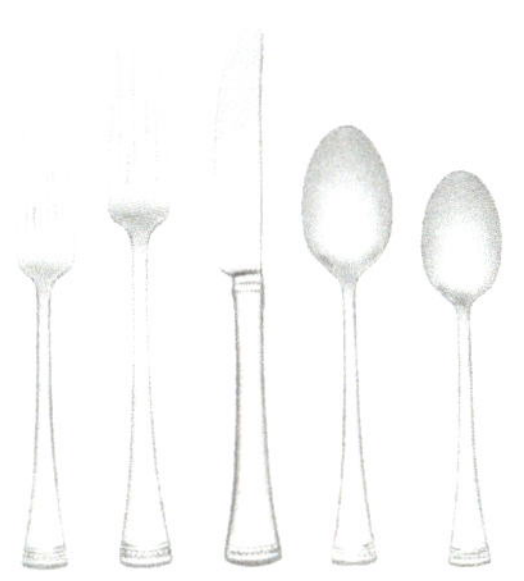

Portola 65 Piece Place Setting
815486

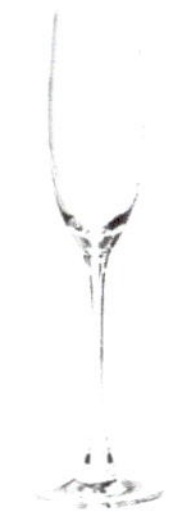

Tuscany Classics Fluted Champagne s/4
6099840

Opal Innocence Silver Place Setting Bowl
850971

July: *Fourth of July Lunch*

Entertain 365 Square Dinner Plate
851519

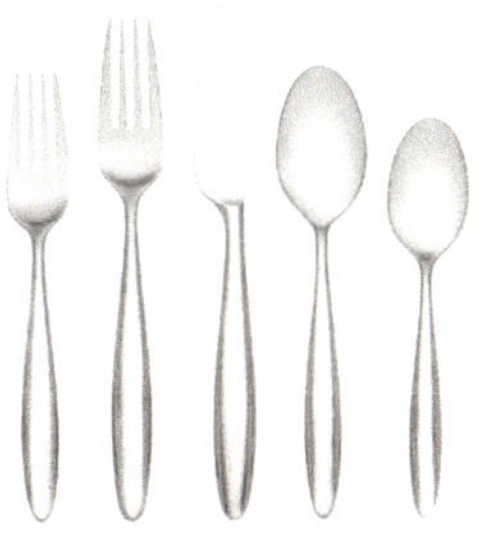

Curve 5 Piece Place Setting
823594

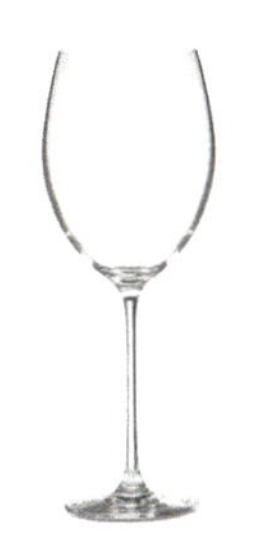

Tuscany Classic Collection
Grand Bordeaux s/4
6099790

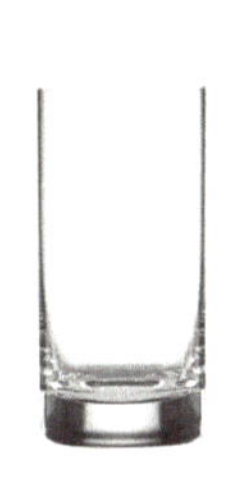

Tuscany Classics
Cylinder Hiball s/4
852914

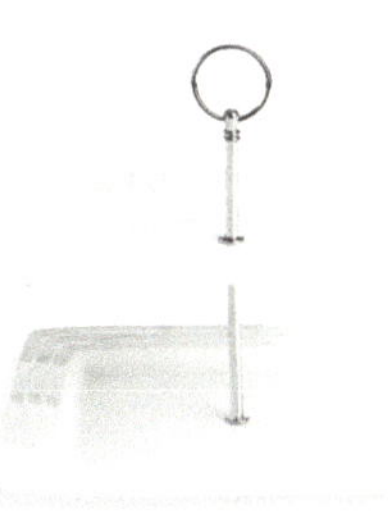

Entertain 365 2-Tier Server
851457

August: *Picnic in the Park*

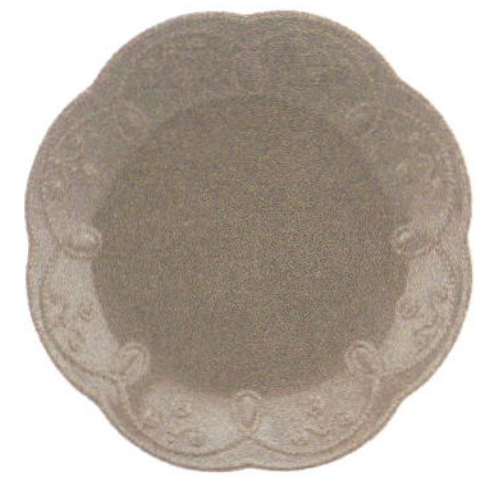

French Perle Latte/ Cherry/ White/Ice Blue/
Violet Dinner Plates
843827, 853855, 822940, 824404, 854741

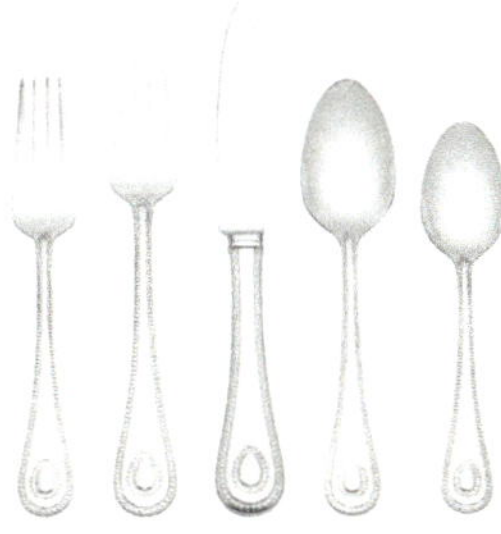

French Perle 65 Piece Place Setting
829739

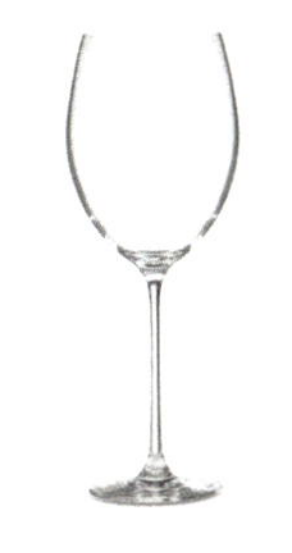

Tuscany Classic Collection
Grand Bordeaux s/4
6099790

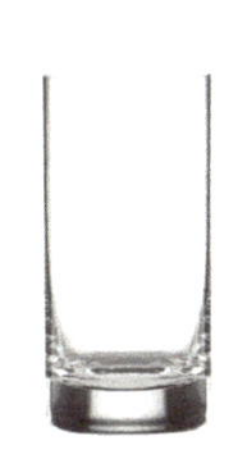

Tuscany Classics
Cylinder Hiball s/4
852914

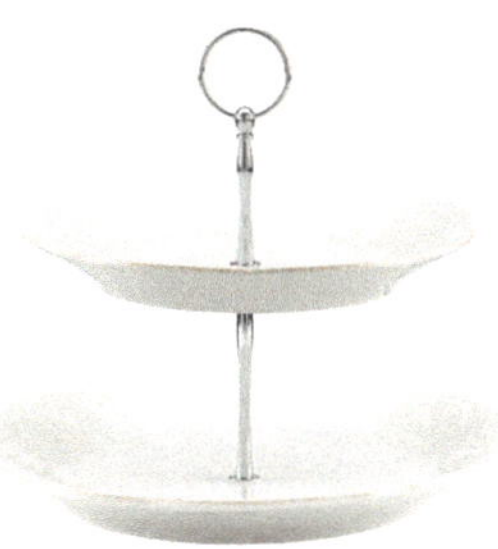

French Perle 2-Tier Server
844453

September: *Labor Day Cocktail Hour*

Passion Bloom Dinner Plate
Passion Bloom Accent Plate
869021, 869017

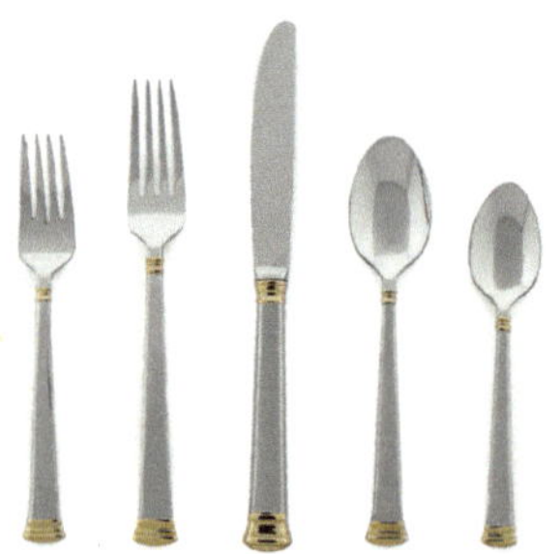

Eternal Gold 5 Piece Place Setting
9828092

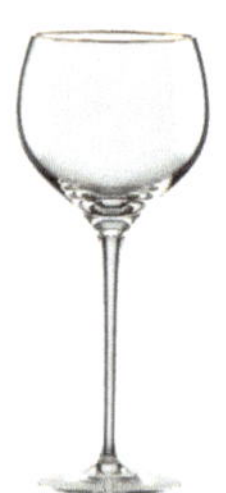

Eternal Gold
Signature Wine
818327

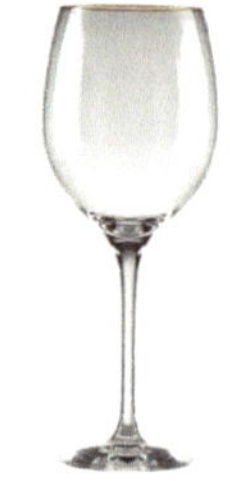

Eternal Gold Signature
All Purpose Beverage
818325

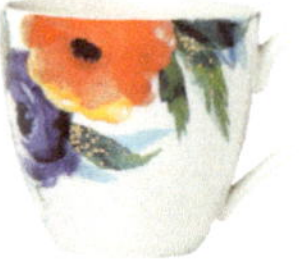

Passion Bloom Coffee Cup
869019

October: *Fall Harvest Dinner*

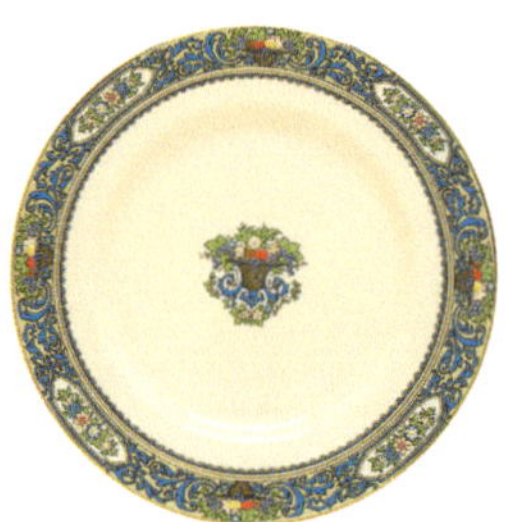

Autumn Dinner Plate
116801000

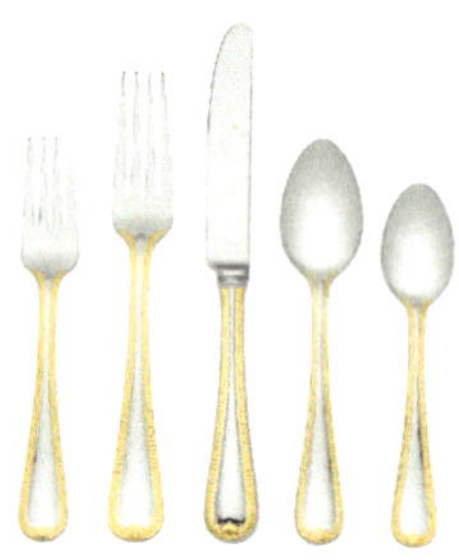

Vintage Jewel Gold 5 Piece Place Setting
6056188

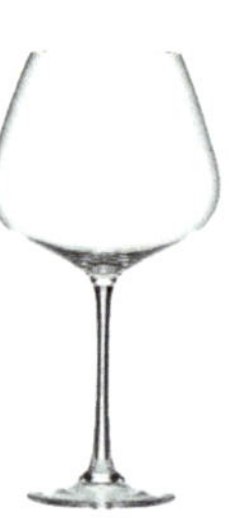

Tuscany Classic
Burgundy s/4
825838

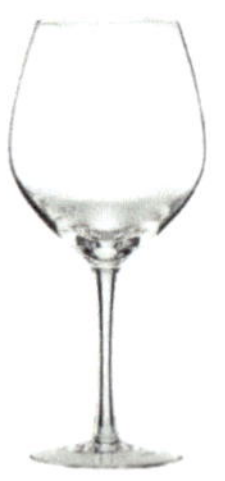

Tuscany Classics
Red Wine Glass s/6
831664

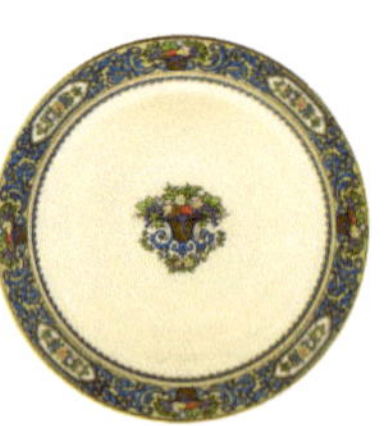

Autumn Pasta / Rim Soup Bowl
6041081

November: *Thanksgiving Dinner*

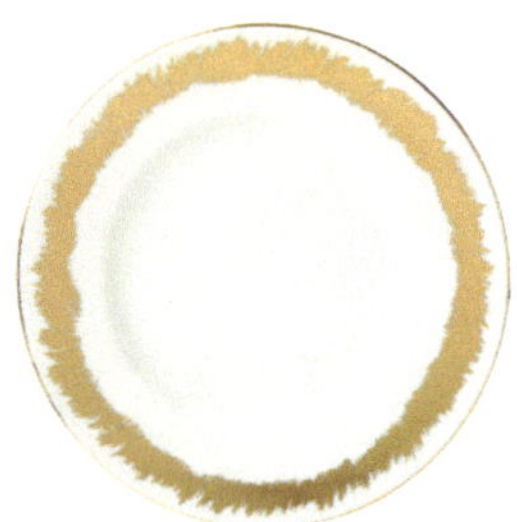

Casual Radiance Dinner Plate
869053

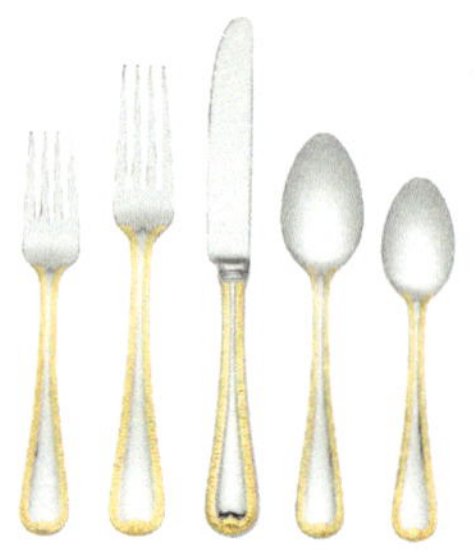

Vintage Jewel Gold 5 Piece Place Setting
6056188

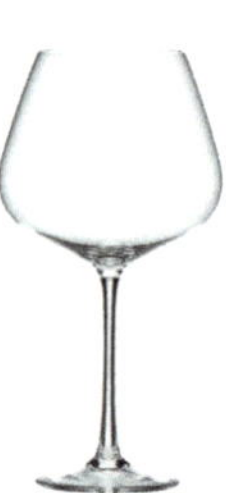

Tuscany Classic
Burgundy s/4
825838

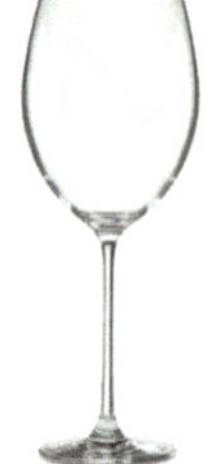

Tuscany Classic Collection
Grand Bordeaux s/4
6099790

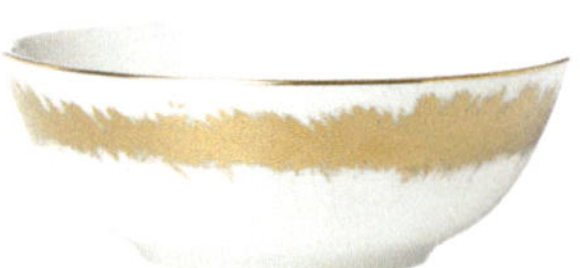

Casual Radiance Place Setting Bowl
869057

December: *Christmas Day Dinner*

Holiday Dinner Plate
146504000

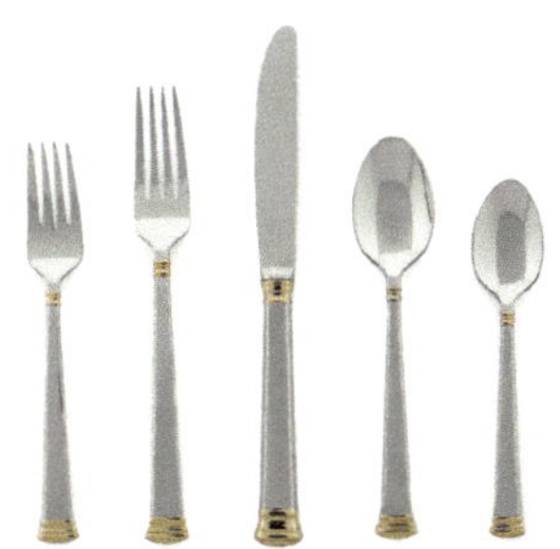

Eternal Gold 5 Piece Place Setting
9828092

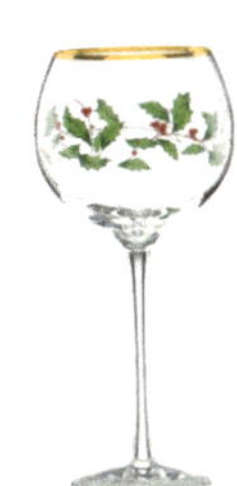

Holiday Balloons
856101

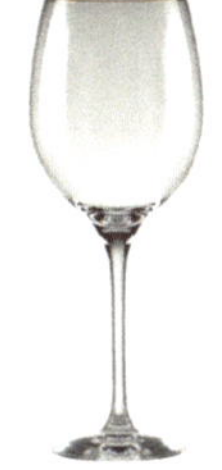

Eternal Gold Signature
All Purpose Beverage
818325

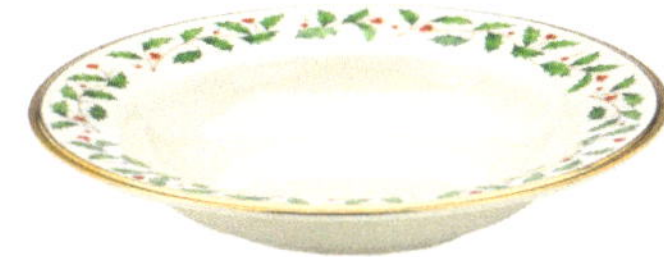

Holiday Pasta / Rim Soup Bowl
146504250

January: *New Year's Day Dinner*

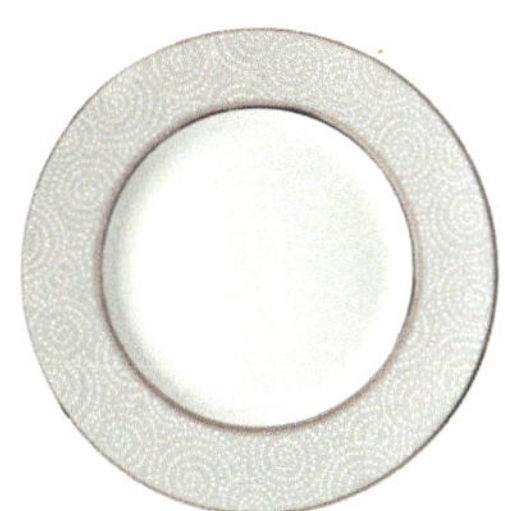

Pearl Beads Dinner Plate
830079

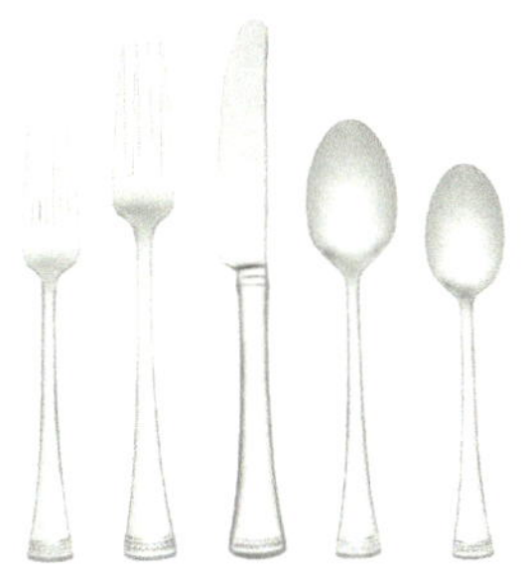

Portola 65 Piece Place Setting
815486

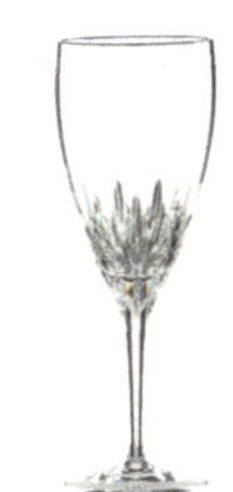

Firelight Platinum Signature
All Purpose Beverage
818213

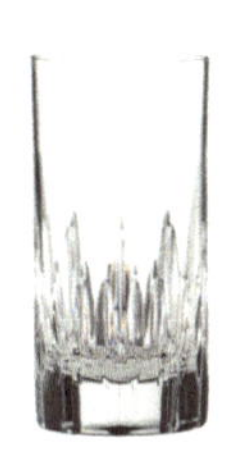

Firelight Platinum
Signature Hiball
854454

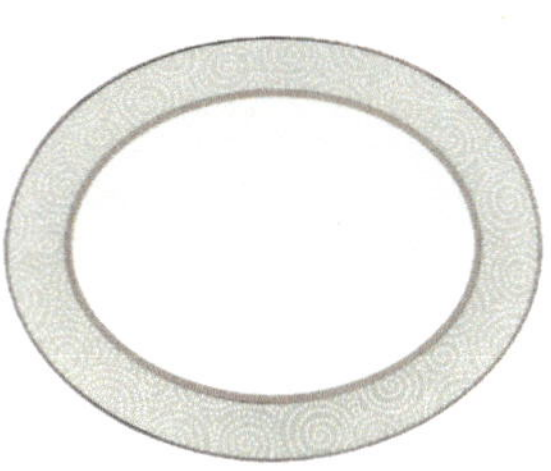

Pearl Beads Platter
830080

February: *Sunday Dinner*

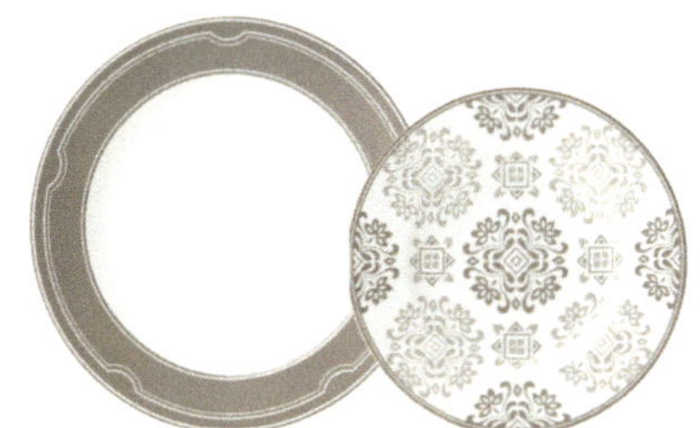

Neutral Party Medallion Dinner Plate
Neutral Party Medallion Accent Plate
867872, 867870

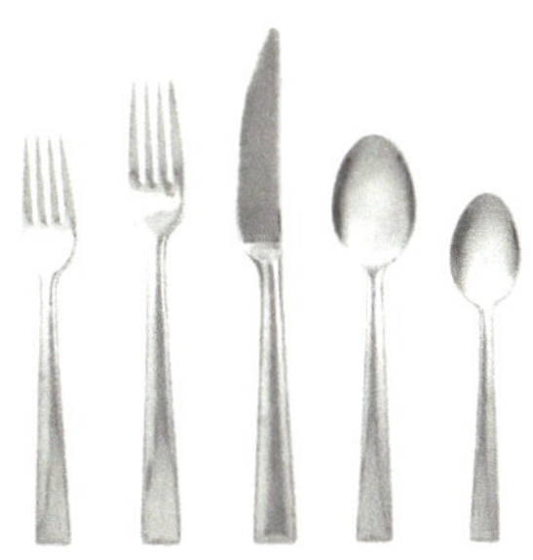

Continental Dining 5 Piece Place Setting
6205264

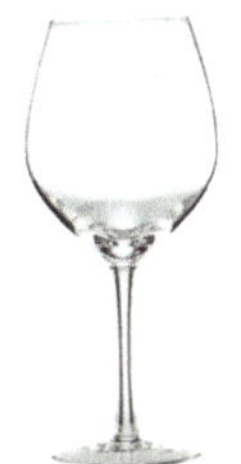

Tuscany Classics
Red Wine s/6
831664

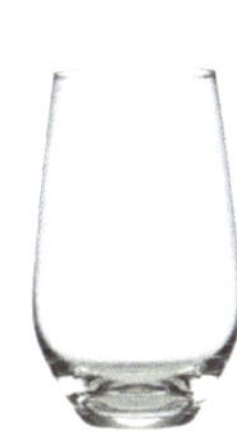

Tuscany Classics
New Hiball s/4
833647

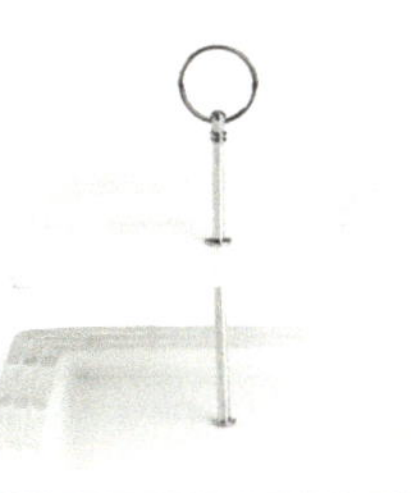

Entertain 365 2-Tier Server
851457

Appendix: Wine Summaries

Wine pairings were recommended by a wine expert and descriptions inspired by various wine distributors and wine publications.

Spring

March: Easter Brunch

Vanilla Puddin Chardonnay – California – Crisp Asian pear and tropical fruit flavors balanced with vanilla and buttery notes.

River Road Pinot Noir Stephanie's Russian River Valley – Russian River Valley, Sonoma, California – Features black cherry and raspberry cream aromas and flavors. Subtle oak overtones can be found on the silky, elegant finish.

Dr Heidemanns Doctorberg Spatlese Riesling – Mosel-Saar-Ruwer, Germany – Packed with apricot, lime and honey notes with dazzling acid structure, rich and harmonious.

April: Springtime Brunch

Conundrum White – California – Unique blend of Viognier, Muscat, Sauvignon Blanc and Chardonnay, focusing on pear, peach and melon.

Le Canon De Cote Montpezat Rosé – Bordeaux, France – A full-bodied blend of 60% merlot and 40% cabernet franc with fresh florals and berries.

Mauro Sebaste Moscato d'Asti – Asti, Piedmont, Italy – A subtle and delicious Moscato, with an intensely fruity note which is aromatic. The sweet flavor is beautifully balanced with the low alcohol and the acidity gives it an appealing freshness.

May: Mother's Day Brunch

Sanrocchetto Verdicchio Jesi White Wine – Castelli di Jesi, Marches, Italy – This medium-bodied white is crisp and dry with a light elegant aroma and flavor. Hints of grapefruit and peaches lead toward a fine finish.

Sobon Estate Viognier White Wine – Amador, California – Aromas of fresh Sierra meadow flowers, with a hint of peach and honeysuckle. The flavors are rich and spicy, full-bodied and richly textured with a lingering finish.

Terre Rouge Muscat Petits Grains – Sierra Foothills, California – Not overly sweet, great with fresh berries or a pear tart with ginger and almonds.

Summer

June: Romantic Dinner at the Beach

Vara Garnacha Rosado Rioja DOC – New Mexico – A beautiful rosado with scents of strawberries and cherries, with light citrus and floral tones. It's a dry wine with a refreshing and elegant taste. It's very attractive and balanced.

Patz & Hall Chardonnay Dutton Ranch – Russian River, Sonoma, California – Fragrant, tropical aromatics underlined by a crisp mineral character. Creamy and succulent, the finish flows gracefully to lingering flavors of lemon cream and white peach.

Champagne Mailly Grand Cru "O" de Mailly – Brut Millesime, Champagne, France – Dry side of brut, is fresh and fruity while also finely textured.

Inniskillin Ice Wine Cabernet Franc – Niagra, Ontario, Canada – Amazing depth of color and outstanding red berry flavors, particularly strawberry.

July: Fourth of July Lunch

Hugues Beauvignac Picpoul White Wine – Picpoul de Pinet, Southern France – A great everyday wine. This dry selection offers relatively low alcohol content and ripe citrus herbal flavors.

Sobon Rezerve Zinfandel – Amador, California – This wine's intense structure, fruit and tannins come together in a fantastic mixture of black pepper, blackberry, earth and chocolate.

Offley 10 Year Tawny Port – Portugal – The creamy caramel flavors are framed by hints of vanilla and spice. There is plenty of dried fruit character running throughout the palate to add to the myriad flavors and scents of this wine.

August: Picnic in the Park

Framingham Marlborough Sauvignon Blanc – Marlborough, New Zealand – This comes from estate vineyards in Wairau along with purchased fruit from the same area. Scents of floral passion fruit yet dry and structured.

Clos St Michel Chateauneuf-du-Pape Blanc – Chateauneuf-du-Pape, Rhone, France – Hints of white currant, white flowers, citrus blossom and vanilla.

Bridgman Riesling – Columbia Valley, Washington – Flavors of juicy peach, guava, mandarin orange, and ripe pineapple on the finish. Bright acidity with a clean finish.

Fall

September: Labor Day Cocktail Hour

Domaine Chenevieres Chablis Les Grandes Vignes – Chablis, Burgundy, France – Fresh and mineral wine, with flavors of green fruits (green apple, kiwi).

Belle Glos Pinot Noir Clark & Telephone – Santa Maria Valley, Santa Barbara, California – A distinctive mix of raspberry and huckleberry flavors, shaded by smoky, toasty oak with lingering flavors of herb and black olive.

October: Fall Harvest Dinner

Dr Heidemanns Graacher Kabinett Riesling – Germany – Scents of pressed apple, summer peaches, and pear melding with smoked nuts and earth. This dry Riesling has a brisk acidity that keeps it refreshing.

Renieri Brunello di Montalcino Riserva Sangiovese – Brunello di Montalcino, Tuscany, Italy Soft oak tones of tobacco, smoke and baking spice that sit heavy over black fruit, tar and licorice.

Osborne Tawny Port – Port, Portugal – Amber in color, with spicy, caramel aromas. Full of nutty, earthy dried fruit flavors, with a touch of wood. Tawny ports are lighter in body, nuttier and less sweet than ruby ports.

November: Thanksgiving Dinner

Tesoro della Regina Pinot Grigio – Valdadige, Veneto, Italy – Crisp apple and peach notes combine with hints of fresh orchard blossoms and a mineral in the background.

Adams Bench Reckoning Merlot – Columbia Valley, Washington – Fresh, vibrant, packed with plum, spice, and herb flavors—fine tannins on the finish.

Quinta das Carvalhas Reserva Tawny Port – Portugal – Smells of baked plum, sweet cherry tart and brick flavors that are rich and well balanced.

Winter

December: Christmas Day Dinner

Allegrini Amarone della Valpolicella Classico Red Wine – Valpolicella, Veneto, Italy – Aromas of black plum, black cherry, black pepper, cinnamon, nutmeg, vanilla, and grilled herbs.

Jemrose Viognier Egret White Wine – Sonoma, California – Floral, apricot marmalade and tropical fruit notes.

Mailly 'Delice' Demi-Sec Grand Cru Champagne – Demi-Sec, Champagne, France – A sumptuous palate of caramel, gingerbread and tree fruits with an aromatic note of nuts and fall spice.

January: New Year's Day Dinner

Montaudon Classe 'M' Champagne – Champagne, France – Full bodied and packed with ripe fruit: white fruits and apricot.

Chateau Kirwan Margaux Bordeaux Blend – 3rd Growth, Margaux, Bordeaux, France – Firm and powerful, a complete wine [BARREL SCORE 92–94].

Marchese dell'Elsa Moscato d'Asti – Asti, Piedmont, Italy – A soft, fruit-driven crowd-pleaser with aromas of peach blossoms and fresh citrus, this delicious white will pair perfectly with fresh fruit.

February: Sunday Dinner

Macchia Zinfandel Adventurous – Amador, California – A bold full-wine with spicy-pepper end notes and a luscious texture.

Amadieu Romane Machotte Gigondas Red Wine – Gigondas, Rhone, France – Red berry (raspberry and cherry), floral scents along with allspice and succulent herbs.

Chateau de la Roulerie Coteaux du Layon Chenin Blanc – Anjou, Loire, France – Blood orange, ginger, fig and glazed peach aromas with apricot notes.

About the Author

Kristal Damron is the owner of Reward Your Appetite Catering, a fine dining catering company committed to providing exquisite culinary dishes with exemplary service.

Kristal is also a finance professional. For over 20 years, corporate finance has been a big part of her life. What she has accomplished in corporate finance has helped her to be successful in this new endeavor. Kristal has a Bachelor of Liberal Arts and Masters of Business Administration from the University of Illinois at Urbana-Champaign. She graduated, with honors, from the Arizona Culinary Institute in Scottsdale, Arizona.

She lives in Phoenix, Arizona, with her husband, Jared, and their two daughters, Arianna Victoria and Alexandria Isabella. She and her family enjoy traveling, visiting parks and museums, and spending time with family and friends.

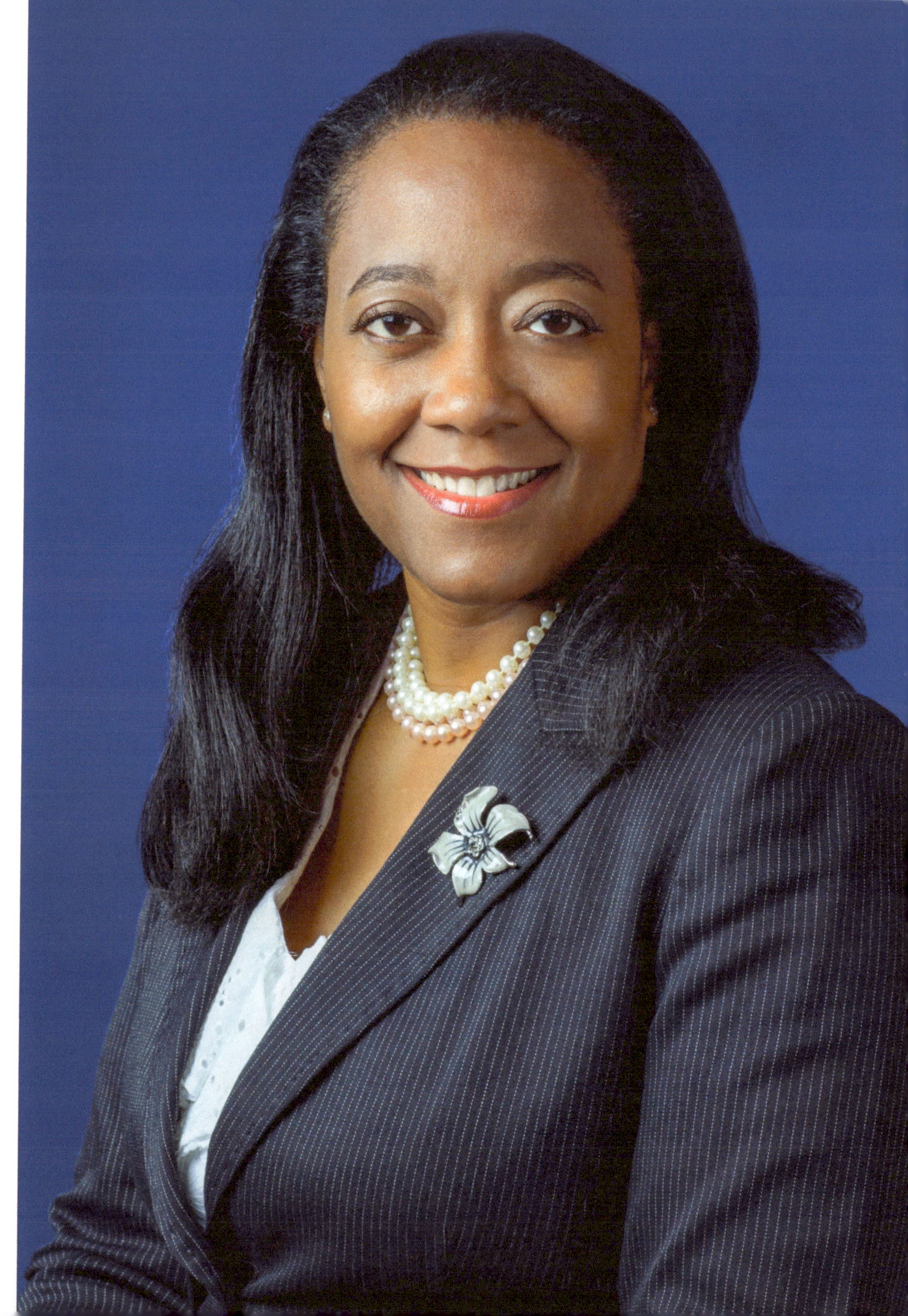

Acknowledgments

Thank you to the many consultants and suppliers for your patience, creativity, and expertise for assisting me in executing my vision for this book. –Kristal

Monthly celebration table setting china, stemware, and flatware provided by Lenox Corporation.

Monthly celebration table setting linens provided by Y Knot Party & Rentals.

Monthly celebration table settings and selected photos photographed by Ivan Martinez Photography.

Monthly celebration table settings floral arrangements created by LUX Wedding Florist.

Food, family, and friends photographed by Your Buddy Patton Photography.

Selected monthly celebration table setting Photo Stylist: Abby Ripes.

Monthly celebration table settings Art Director: Negin Keyhanfar.

Monthly celebration venues: Chateau de Vie, Ocotillo Golf Course, Fullerton Ranch Ramada, Everton and Gayle Ifill, and Aldea Weddings at The Landmark.

Manuscript Editor (Developmental and Copy): Carolyn Bond.

Proofreaders: Mark Lange, Natascha Bohmann.

Book Design: ps:studios.

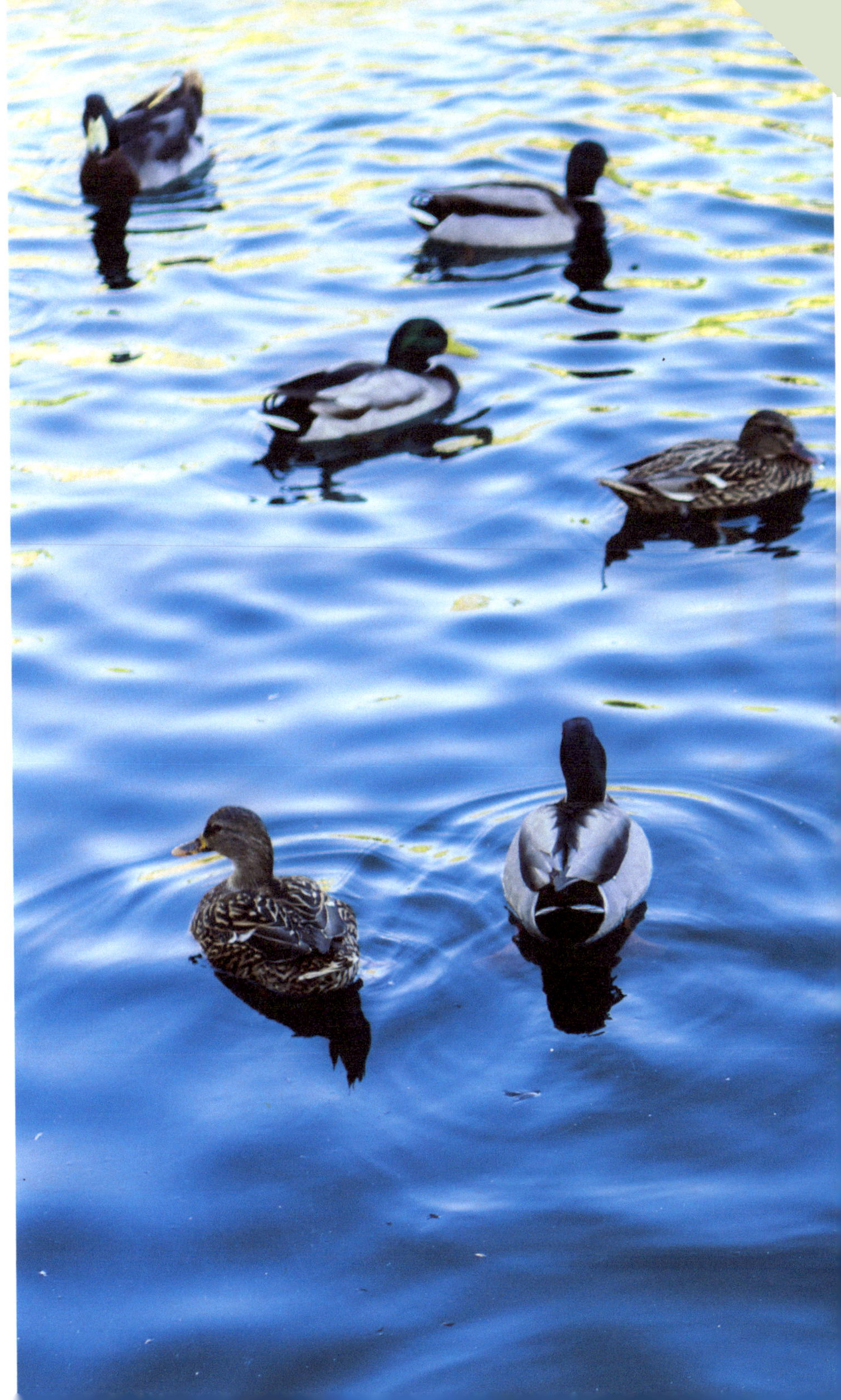

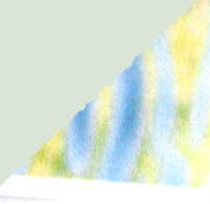

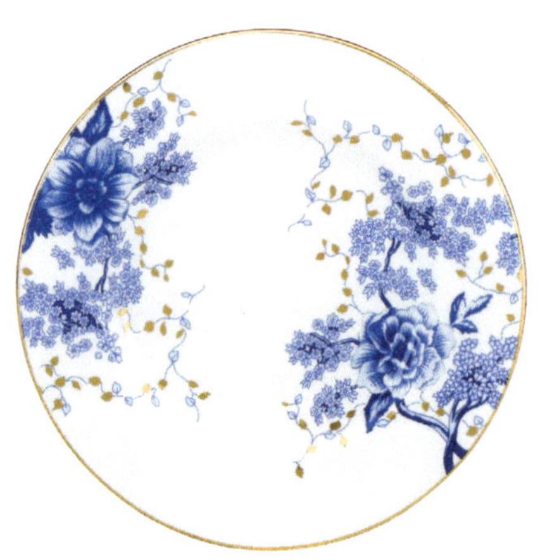

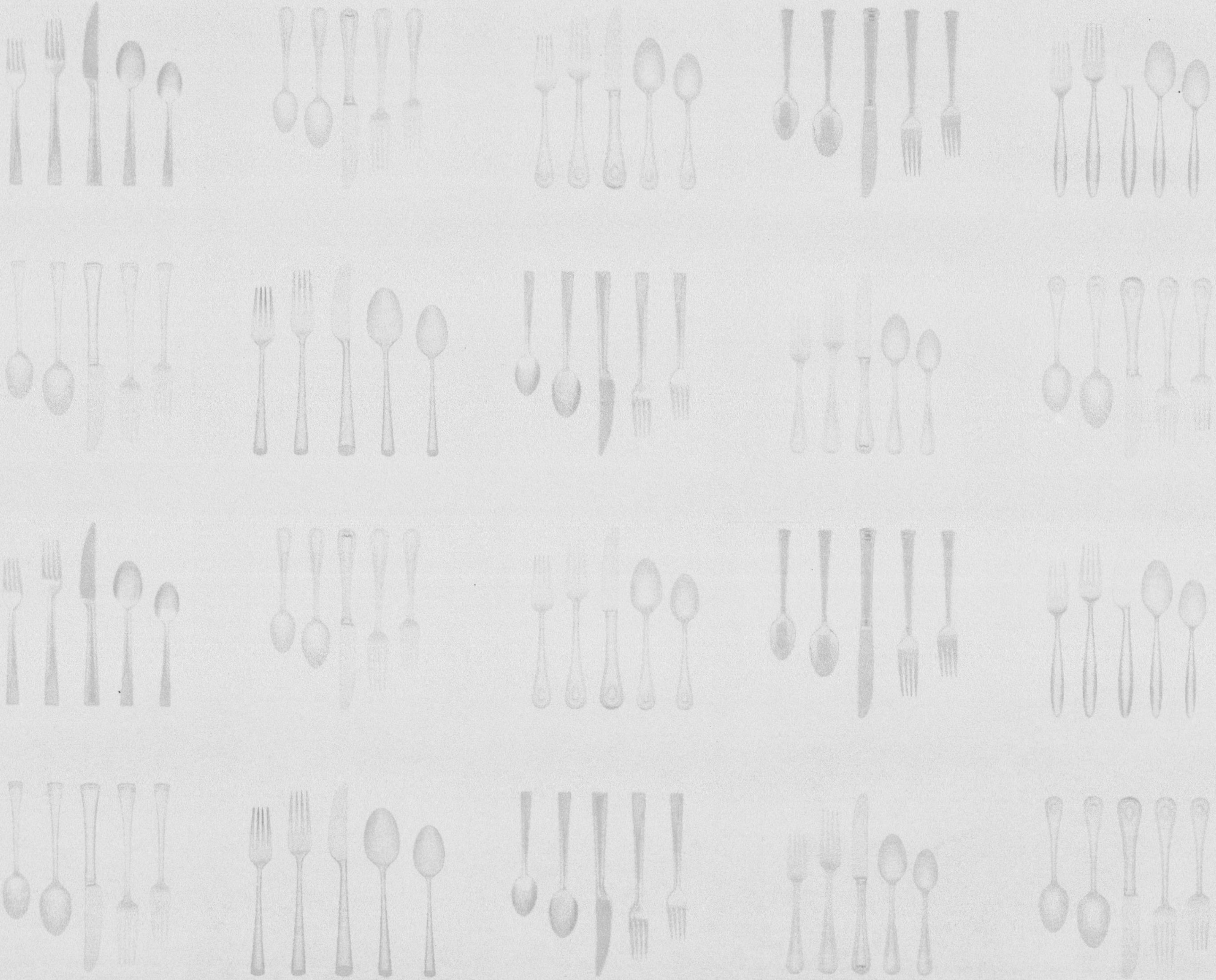